Praise for *Get a Grip on Your Grammar*

"I know about as much about grammar as I do about kite surfing, but Kris Spisak's delightful, breezy take has dark powers that give a rookie like me fingers instead of left thumbs, light instead of fog."

—Kevin Smokler, author of *Brat Pack America* and *Practical Classics*

A Grammar Book for Those Who Hate Grammar

GET A GRIP ON YOUR GRAMMAR

250
WRITING AND EDITING
REMINDERS FOR THE CURIOUS
OR CONFUSED

KRIS SPISAK

This edition first published in 2017 by Career Press, an imprint of
Red Wheel/Weiser, LLC
With offices at:
65 Parker Street, Suite 7
Newburyport, MA 01950
www.redwheelweiser.com
www.careerpress.com

ISBN: 978-1-63265-091-7
Library of Congress Cataloging-in-Publication Data available upon request.]

Interior by PerfecType, Nashville, TN
Typeset in Gotham, Adobe Caslon Pro

Printed in the United States of America
IBI
10 9 8 7 6 5 4 3 2 1

DEDICATION

For Frank,
who always likes knowing the precise rules of the game.

ACKNOWLEDGMENTS

When I first started jotting down my writing tips for my editing clients on my blog, I never guessed at the project it would become. There are more people to thank than I can name here, and you know who you are; however, I want to express my deepest gratitude especially to Katharine Herndon, Phillip Hilliker, Josh Watson, Kathryn Hively, Zachary Steele, Ricki Schultz, Lisa Hagan, my family, and the endlessly supportive community of James River Writers.

CONTENTS

INTRODUCTION

Just like thinking before we speak, if we think before we write, the world can be a better place. Don't you think?

Jobs are lost for typos on resumes. Friends lose respect for each other over social media posts. Feuds between neighbors begin over the placement of apostrophes on backyard grill invitations. Semicolons cry themselves to sleep at night because no one understands them. The ever-popular ellipsis has an ego the size of an asterisk. (Too far?)

Maybe it's the fluid nature of the language; maybe we've never been taught; maybe we've just never cared. Whatever the source of our grammatical predicament, it's time to roll up our sleeves, folks.

We're not all poets or novelists, but we are all writers. We email; we text; we post on social media; we craft memos and reports, menus and outdoor signage, birthday cards and sticky notes on the fridge. Everyone needs reminders about proper English writing rules, and the answer to this dilemma isn't as tedious as you might think. I'm not suggesting sentence diagramming parties or subject-verb agreement dating games. I get that the vocabulary of grammarians can be as intimidating as computer code: misplaced modifiers, subordinating conjunctions, appositives, comma splices, dependent clauses . . . (Hang on, dear readers! I didn't mean to lose you in a single line!)

Personally, I like to keep things simple. Grammarian jargon isn't necessary for comprehending correct language use. Sure, the English language is not always logical. There are words that are so gosh darn similar, it's hard to remember which one is which—or a witch (cackle, cackle). There are hard rules and then a heck of a lot of exceptions. I get it. I truly do. That's why I've written this book.

No matter where you go and what you do in your life, putting down words skillfully and correctly will take you further (note, not "farther" unless cars start running on language, which would be pretty cool, actually. Who can I get on that?).

Putting a disclaimer on emails from your smartphone is not enough. We owe it to ourselves and to everyone who sees our written words to get it right.

All right?

Word Usage

We live in a fast-paced time, but that's no excuse for typing drunkenly across keyboards. Sometimes we know the rules and abandon them; sometimes, we err because we don't know any better. Consider this your call-to-action. No more excuses. Use your words precisely. It's my challenge to you.

What follows in this section is my list of 153 commonly confused words. I may not offer answers to the universe, but I can at least talk you through the differences between "literally" and "figuratively," "lay" and "lie," and "disinterested" and" "uninterested." Curious? Read on!

Writing Tip #1: "A" vs. "An"

This one seems so obvious. Why, you might ask, am I even taking the time to talk about something you clearly learned in 1st grade? Well, my friends, the English language is full of exceptions—and many of the "a" vs. "an" exceptions are overlooked time and time again.

When you see a horse with a long horn upon its head, is it "a unicorn" or "an unicorn"? When you make a mistake, do you call it "an honest error" or "a honest error"? First reactions may say that "an" is always the article used before words starting with vowels, and "a" is before words starting with consonants; however, here are those tricky exceptions I was talking about.

Stop thinking purely spelling with the a/an rule. Think about the sound. In most cases, if it sounds like it starts with a vowel, go with the "an"; otherwise, "a" is a likely bet.

You need to use "an" before an unsounded "h," as in "honest," "hour," or "honor." You need to use "a" before words that start with the letter "u," in cases where the sound echoes a "y," as in "unicorn," "union," and "ukulele."

It's a simple rule, but people confuse it all the time.

Writing Tip #2: "Accept" vs. "Except"

The English language is full of exceptions that we have to accept. Should we dub them "acceptions" (exceptions that you have to accept even when they annoy you)? Okay, maybe I made that up, and maybe it's not as clever as it was in my head. Let's stick to basics here. There is a clear difference between "accept" and "except," and it's more than just the first two letters.

- Accept (think "acceptance") is a verb meaning "to consent to receive something" or "to come to see something as suitable, valid, or right."
- Except (think "exception") is a preposition meaning "not including" or "other than," or it's a verb meaning "to exclude" or "to omit."

I'm pretty sure we know the difference and simply write too quickly sometimes. I'm pretty sure. That's what I tell myself anyhow. You surely won't make that mistake anymore, right?

———

Writing Tip #3: "Adapt" vs. "Adopt"

"Adaptation" and "adoption" are easy enough to tell apart, but when used in their verb forms, "adapt" and "adopt" often become quite confusing. Are you an early adapter or early adopter? Do you adapt to your surroundings by adopting a watch-out-world attitude?

For a quick refresher:

- "Adapt" means to modify or to make suitable for certain conditions.
- "Adopt" means to select or take as one's own, be it an idea or a child.

Although they are indeed quite similar, they come from different Latin roots. "Adapt" comes from *adaptare*, which translates as "to fit." "Adopt" comes from *adoptare*, which translates as "to choose." The similarity of these words even in Latin makes me wonder how long people have been confused by them. Did Homer ever slip up? I'll tell myself no, but the world never will know.

If you want to take this a step further, we can even discuss "adept" and "apt," which are often jumbled in this confusing mix.

- "Adept" is an adjective meaning very skilled.
- "Apt" is an adjective meaning either being quick to learn, suited for a purpose, or to be likely to do something.

These A-P-T words will keep you on your toes, for sure.

As for those "early adapters," they probably have set their alarm clocks a few hours ahead of you so that they can have time to spend in their workshop tweaking their inventions. "Early adopters" are the group who are first to embrace a new technology or idea.

Writing Tip #4: "Addition" vs. "Edition"

When a new edition of a book comes out, it might make for an addition to your bookshelves, but the meanings of these words shouldn't be complicated for you. If you think of the word "add," you'll always use the correct word.

- "Addition" is only concerned with adding, whether referring to something being added or the process of adding.
- "Edition" has a few definitions. Bookworms like me automatically think of "editions" of a book or specifically updated versions, often with new or enhanced information; "edition" also means the format in which a work is published or a later version of something.

But, again, this one is simple. As long as you remember "addition" is all about "adding," you'll never go wrong again.

Writing Tip #5: "Adverse" vs. "Averse"

Sometimes a single letter pops up to wreak havoc, and in this case, it's the letter "d." Even if their definitions don't immediately jump to your mind, you know deep down that "adverse" and "averse" are not positive words. Perhaps there's something about them both that leaves a bad taste in your mouth. Maybe that's why you never bothered to learn them or their differences.

All together now, let's take a deep breath. There's nothing wrong with learning these definitions correctly.

- "Adverse" means unfavorable, antagonistic, or being in a contrary direction. One of this word's most common usages is "adverse effects."
- "Averse" means to have strong feelings of repugnance or opposition.

I know a lot of people who are averse to using autocorrect on their smartphones because it ends up causing more typos than it saves. Then again, we could talk about the adverse effects of spell-check and auto-correct on a generation's spelling abilities, and oh, the fun we would have. Yes, I said fun. What? Are you averse to this idea?

Writing Tip #6: "Advice" vs. "Advise"

Mark Twain once said, "The dream vocabulary shaves meanings finer and closer than do the world's daytime dictionaries." I love this concept, but then again, some people have nonsensical dreams. It's in the dream vocabulary of these eccentric individuals that word pairings like "adviser" and "advisor" must take their roots.

What's the difference between these two? That's a great question. The answer: there is no difference. Don't you hate that?

- "Adviser" is more commonly used and is listed in most dictionaries as the primary spelling.
- "Advisor" only takes the lead when it comes to official job titles (for example, Senior Advisor to the President).

Those of us who like black and white grammar rules will have to remain bothered. Though perhaps another quote attributed to Mark Twain sums it up best: "I don't give a damn for a man that can only spell a word one way." Admittedly, there's a debate whether these words were Twain's, Andrew Jackson's, or someone else's altogether. Whoever it was, though, is perhaps the best adviser of them all.

Writing Tip #7: "Affect" vs. "Effect"

Words that sound similar and look similar are kind of like twins. At first glance, they seem like duplicates, but in the end, a lot of people will be annoyed if you confuse them. Time to stop insulting words, people! Are you using "affect" and "effect" correctly?

- In most situations, "affect" is a verb with "influence" being a close synonym. For example, "Quick communications online have affected people's writing habits."
- In most situations, "effect" is a noun with "result" being a close synonym. For example, "One effect of quick communications online is a proliferation of casual, incorrect writing."

When you affect something, there is an effect.

However, the English language is never that simple—if you even call this description simple. Affect and effect also have other forms, which add confusion. Nine times out of 10, though, follow this guide, and you'll be all set.

Here's where the inquisitive read on. More power to you, grammar-curious friends!

- "Affect" can also be a verb meaning "to make a display of" or "to deliberately cultivate." In addition, "affect" can be a noun (egads!) used by psychiatrists and other social scientists referring to "emotion," but unless you fall into a discipline familiar with this use, I wouldn't recommend it.
- "Effect" has its own complications. It can be a noun of different meanings when discussing your "personal effects" or "sound effects." "Effect" can also be defined as a verb meaning "to create," such as in the sentence, "Grammarians of the world effect change for the better."

Oh, and now I have you staring at word-twins again trying to figure out the difference. Remember the simple definitions first. Subtleties can come later for the brave and/or scientifically minded.

Writing Tip #8: "Aisle" vs. "Isle"

Maybe you've been asked what you'd take along with you to a desert isle. Maybe if they were confused about their spelling, they might have asked you about your choices for a dessert aisle. As for me, I think I'd choose dark chocolate. It answers both questions, really.

Remember:

- An "isle" is an island, sometimes considered to be a small island.
- An "aisle" is a walkway between sections of seats or shelves, such as in a plane, a church, a grocery store, or a movie theatre.

Their origins are as different as their definitions, with "isle" coming from the Latin *insula* and "aisle" coming from the Latin *āla*, so make sure your spelling is accurate—unless you're grocery shopping with Gilligan, that is. The Professor and Mr. Howell might want to be precise, but if you're a grocery shopping castaway, I think even I will give you some leniency.

Writing Tip #9: "A Long" vs. "Along"

When I think of a long tale, I can't help but think of Lewis Carroll's *Alice's Adventures in Wonderland*, where the Dormouse tells a story that is recorded on the page in the shape of a long tail. Sure, there's another word confusion at the root of this reference, but it does indeed depict a long tale in the shape of a long tail, which runs along the page.

Note, as I'm explaining this to you, you have no trouble understanding that "long" is an adjective describing length, and that "a" is simply an article that precedes it. Then why is it that "along" and "a long" are so often confused?

"Along," as you well know, is a preposition, meaning on the course of or over a path or specific direction.

While Tweedle-Dee and Tweedle-Dum were telling Alice about Walruses and Carpenters, for example, all Alice wanted to do was to continue along after the white rabbit. The cards who painted the roses red must have used a long ladder.

And as wild as that story is, I enjoy Alice every time. Don't you?

Writing Tip #10: "All Ready" vs. "Already"

All right, already. Are you all ready to discuss the differences between these two words? Much like the eternal squishing of "all right" into "alright," "all ready" is often forgotten in lieu of "already." The problem is, though, that these are not alternate spellings of the same idea. "All ready" and "already" don't honestly have much to do with each other.

- "All ready" is pretty self-explanatory if you take a moment to think about it. Are you a little bit ready, or are you all ready? Is just one of you ready, or are you all ready? Do you see the slight variations in these two sentences? In short, "all ready" can mean either totally prepared or that a group is prepared.
- "Already," on the other hand, means before this moment or before another specific moment. You already knew this, though, didn't you?

Squeezing "all ready" into "already" is not an acceptable contraction, so stop doing it already. Got it?

Writing Tip #11: "Allude" vs. "Refer"

Some people are direct in their conversation. Other people are more subtle. Some people will give you a list of exactly what they want for their birthday. Other people prefer to drop hints. When you think of "allude" and "refer," think of these different types of people. It will help explain their differences.

Contrary to what you may think, to "allude" to something is different from "referring" to it.

- "To allude" means to hint or indirectly suggest to something.
- "To refer" means to make a direct reference to or point about something.

"Refer" is the friend who emails you a hyperlink to an item and a coupon code that expires in the next few days. There is no question about what he wants or how quickly you should act. "Allude" is a bit more circumspect. She might circle something in a catalog and leave it out where others can see or remark how great something is without directly saying she wants it. Whether "refer" is rude or straight-to-the-point or whether "allude" is tactful or too subtle to be understood is beyond the point. The key is seeing their differences and understanding that each have their ways.

"Allude" and "refer" are not synonyms. Please stop using them as such.

Writing Tip #12: "All Together" vs. "Altogether"

All together now, say it with me: "all together" and "altogether" are two different words. I know some of you prefer one or the other, but it's time to focus hard and get this right.

I suppose I shouldn't be altogether shocked at this confusion—I remember the day I learned this one myself—but let's break it down once and for all.

When you learned to spell "together," did you learn to spell it by remembering the breakdown of "to get her"? I always thought it was a bit menacing, but maybe that's why it stuck in my head. Let's use the same logic when remembering "all together."

If we're all going to get her, we need to go all together.

Remember:

- "All together" means to be collected as a group.
- "Altogether" is an adverb that means entirely or on the whole.

Meanwhile, I'm altogether disturbed by this threatening writing tip, so I want to end with a casual reminder to give your mom, sister, grandma, or best gal pal a call. Maybe even buy her flowers or tickets to a baseball game just because. (Yes, I said a baseball game. Who doesn't love peanuts and Cracker Jacks?)

Writing Tip #13: "Allusion" vs. "Illusion" vs. "Elusion"

Most people feel pretty comfortable around the word illusion. Whether it makes them think of David Copperfield or Edward Norton is up to the individual. I think the word "allusion" reminds a lot of people of their high school English classes and the subtleties of texts they may or may not have ever read. The word "allusion" often brings to mind pop quizzes and red pens, and I think that needs to end now.

- An "allusion" alludes. In case that isn't helpful, either refer to the difference between "refer" and "allude" in Writing Tip #11 or let me explain further. If you've ever read between the lines, you've picked up on an allusion or a subtle reference.

- An "illusion," of course, is something that isn't perceived correctly by the senses. Sometimes, it's a trick of the eyes (that is, an optical illusion), a thrown voice, or a rabbit pulled out of a hat. An illusion can also be something false or deceptive.
- Just to keep you on your toes, an "elusion" is an act of evading or avoiding capture.

These words make me think of "The Name Game" gone awry. Fee-fi-fo-fusion. Allusion. But however you think of them, be sure to think of them correctly.

Writing Tip #14: "Alot" vs. "A Lot" vs. "Allot"

"Alot" isn't a word, people. Save your writing dignity (and the headaches of the grammar-picky) and add a space in there. It's not that hard. Look, I just did it. There, I did it a few more times. Wow, I'm awesome at this. Okay, I digress.

- If you like something bunches, you like it a lot. Two words. A lot.
- Allot is indeed a word, meaning "to give or to allocate a share of something," but I'm pretty sure that's not the one you're misspelling.

Unless it's a hashtag, put that space in there. We'll all be the better for it. #Grammarrocks #alot

Writing Tip #15: "Alter" vs. "Altar"

If you're going to the chapel to get married and you're thinking about either "alter" or "altar," I hope for the sake of your marriage that you're thinking of the holy structure at the front of the church. If, by chance, you're thinking about the other form of the word, the form that is connected to "alternative" and "alteration," I wonder if that walk down the aisle is the best choice for you at the moment.

One little vowel can make all the difference in writing these words correctly. Remember:

- "Alter" means change.
- "Altar" means the holy structure upon which offerings are presented. They are commonly found in churches, shrines, temples, and other places of worship.

If you've ever made this mistake, you wouldn't be the first. In fact, the word "altar" is derived from the Middle English word *alter* and the Old English *altar*, which was derived from the Latin *altāre*, meaning a place to sacrifice to the gods. Its roots are also related to the Latin word *altus*, which means high.

"Alter," alternatively, comes from the French word *alterer*, which was derived from the Medieval Latin word *alterare*, both of which mean to change.

In other words, the spelling difference between these two words has been causing some confusion for some time. I just hope that confusion isn't happening at the front of a church. And if it is, good luck with that.

Writing Tip #16: "Alright" vs. "All Right"

Maybe you had a teacher who once told you, "Alright is not all right." The rule still stands, though in the ever-evolving world of words, "alright" seems to be gaining traction—in British English especially, according to the experts. But in nine out of 10 dictionaries, "alright" is considered a misspelling of "all right."

This common error is seemingly rooted in language patterns used in words such as "already" and "altogether"; however, the two-word form is the standard you should use when you want to appear like you know what you're doing. And we all like to appear like we know what we're doing on occasion, right?

As for that 10th dictionary, it speaks of two different definitions, where "alright" means simply satisfactory, whereas "all right" means correct in its adjective form. According to this logic, these two statements have two different meanings:

> Example 1: "My exam was all right." (It was all correct. No mistakes!)
> Example 2: "My exam was alright." (It was okay. I probably passed.)

It's words like these that make the evolution of language and its accepted use an interesting subject to follow. Nonetheless, until more dictionaries accept "alright" as a correct spelling, I suggest you use the two-word form in more formal communications. All right?

Writing Tip #17: "Aloud" vs. "Out loud"

"LOL" (laughing out loud) may be ubiquitous these days, but why not "LA" (laughing aloud)? Is there a difference? It's shorter—and we love shorter in this era of texts and Twitter—so was it the city of Los Angeles that held it back?

Here's the nitty gritty on these two words. The original form, which dates back to the thirteenth century, is "aloud," but in the early 1800s, "out loud" appeared as a colloquialism. Why? Who knows. But in our day of "totes," "forevs," and "awesomesauce," we can understand weird things happening with language.

Most consider "aloud" and "out loud" synonyms, though the die-hards might reserve the original "aloud" for formal writing and "out loud" for casual conversation. "LOL" seems to follow this train of thought. It's definitely an acronym designed for casual use.

So we can't blame Los Angeles for the appearance of "LOL" rather than "LA." Who knew text-speak considered grammar rules?

Writing Tip #18: "Anxious" vs. "Excited"

When you say that you're "anxious" for something, are you saying what you mean to? Are you anxious about a party, about the end of the semester, or to see clowns at the circus?

Please remember that "anxious" is not a synonym of "excited." People often misuse "anxious" in this way, but the true definition has a more negative connotation. When you are slightly nervous about something coming soon, you are anxious. When you are eager about something happening, you are not anxious about it.

Example 1: Samuel was anxious about the clown's arrival at the party. (That is, Samuel wasn't looking forward to it.)

Example 2: Isabella was excited about the clown's arrival at the party. (That is, Isabella was looking forward to it.)

Watch what you say (and write), especially when talking about clowns. People have a lot of strong feelings—in both directions—about clowns.

Writing Tip #19: "Anytime" vs. "Any Time"

"Anytime" is a relatively new word—yes, I'm calling early twentieth century "recent" for the sake of this linguistic argument. And you know that any time there is a new word, there's going to be a grammarian hullaballoo. Here's another example.

"Anytime" (one word) is considered a casual form; it's not one for your resume or emails to advance you up the corporate ladder. In fact, this one-word form is still not recognized by some dictionaries (I'm looking at you, OED). "Anytime" is technically defined as an adverb meaning "whenever" or "on any occasion," but as a new word, it is young and defiant, having other meanings too. "Anytime" can also simply mean "no problem" in response to a "thank you."

If you aren't sure if you can get away with "anytime" versus "any time," ask yourself if you can replace the word in question with "at any time." For example:

When are you free for coffee?

Anytime. (Correct. Answering "at any time" would also make sense.)

Does dinner Tuesday work?

Sure, anytime after six. (Correct. Answering "at any time after six" would also make sense.)

Do you have anytime to take a walk with me? (Incorrect. Do you have "at any time" to take a walk with me doesn't make sense. The adjective-noun pairing "any time" [two words] is needed here.)

I can go further with this one, but I'll stop there.

"Any time" (two words) is admittedly the standard form. If you're ever concerned about which form you should choose, experts argue you'll never go wrong by using the two-word combination. I'm not sure I completely agree with that, but then again, I'm American and therefore a linguistic rebel at heart. Or so the argument goes. (The casual "anytime" is apparently much more common on this side of the Atlantic.)

Personally, do I dare to use the nonstandard form? Anytime I can. Take that, Oxford English Dictionary.

Writing Tip #20: "Anyway" vs. "Anyways" vs. "Any way"

Allow me to let you in on a secret: "anyways" is not actually a word. I'll let that sink into your brain wrinkles. Yes, it's true.

The correct word many of you are looking for is "anyway" without the "s" on the end. "Anyway" is an adverb. Can adverbs be pluralized? No, they cannot be.

- "Anyway" has two major meanings. It means regardless or anyhow, (for example, I know some of you are going to keep using "anyways" anyway), and in more casual use, it acts as a segue, returning to an earlier topic of conversation or back to a major point.
- "Any way" is a matter of whichever path or whatever direction. The easy reminder is that if you can swap out the words "in the" for "any," you should use the two-word form (for example, "I don't recommend you write any way you want to on your resume" would still make sense if the words were swapped: "I don't recommend you write in the way you want to on your resume").

I won't lie. When it comes to "anyways," people have been tacking on that extra "s" for a long time. It's not a recent development, but every time it arises, it never quite gains enough momentum to win over any dictionaries more than a note of slang or casual use. Thus, avoid "anyways" in all formal writing. Maybe you want to avoid it all together.

Anyway, that's my two cents on these two words.

Writing Tip #21: "Appraise" vs. "Apprise"

Have you ever wondered if you had a forgotten heirloom in your attic worth millions? Not that you'd necessarily part with your great-granddaddy's pocket watch, but it's interesting to know its worth either way. If you think of finding this gem and having it appraised, maybe you expect the item to be praised and lauded. Here's your hint when it comes to "appraise" versus "apprise." If you think something could be praised in the process, you need "appraise." Remember:

- "Appraise" is a verb meaning to be assessed to determine value.
- "Apprise" is a verb meaning to make someone aware of something.

Thus, I am apprising you of the differences between "appraise" and "apprise." I am not qualified to appraise much—unless it's good grammar, but that's more precious than gold, isn't it?

Writing Tip #22: "Assent" vs. "Ascent" vs. "A Scent"

At the pearly gates, will St. Peter give his assent for your ascent? I wonder if such a place has a scent. If so, it would have to be something luscious and absolutely perfect. I think it's pancakes—maybe pancakes and coffee. Oh my goodness, does heaven smell like IHOP?

My breakfast cravings aside, are you spelling these words correctly? Remember:

- "Assent" means to agree or approve.
- "Ascent" means to rise upward, either physically or meta-phorically, such as in social status or job position.

- "A scent" is something you smell or something a dog might follow if he is thinking about buttery, syrupy goodness.

I don't know about heavenly ascents, but I do know I give my assent for a breakfast out. Is your stomach grumbling too?

———

Writing Tip #23: "Awhile" vs. "A While"

The trouble with understanding "awhile" versus "a while" is that their meanings are so gosh darn close that it's easy to get it wrong. I hate explaining word choice by arguing purely about parts of speech, but that's largely what's at play in this case.

- "Awhile" is an adverb meaning "for a short time" (for example, they relaxed awhile by the water, and then made dinner).
- "A while" is an article plus a noun referring to a length of time (it's been a while since they visited the lake house).

If you're stuck on which one to use, think about whether you could swap it out for another adverb (for example, they relaxed happily/dramatically/ridiculously by the water). If that doesn't make sense, think about whether you could swap it out for another duration of time (it's been a decade/a day/a year since they visited).

This adverb-noun conundrum baffles, time and time again. But I have faith you can get it right. Understanding may take a while, but you'll get there.

———

Writing Tip #24: "Back up" vs. "Backup"

Hold on, let's back up here. Have you backed up your files? Go back up the stairs and do so right away. There's nothing worse than losing a project you're working on—like your first book, when you're 50 pages in, and your computer gets a virus, on your birthday. (Sigh, I haven't quite gotten over that one yet.)

Personal tangents aside, do you see the differences between "back up" and "backup"? It's more than just a space. We're talking about entirely different definitions:

- "Backup" is a noun that means something or someone that can be used to support or replace another. It can also be used to describe that support or replacement (physical or digital), as well as to name a name of blockage of some sort (for example, a traffic backup).
- "Back up" is a verb that has a few meanings, from moving in a backward direction, to offering the support or replacement functions just discussed, to making a copy of a digital file for the sake of preservation.

In this digital era, "backup" is being used more and more, but because of this increased usage, people are starting to mistype a lot. Some people prefer the space between words in all situations. Others skip the space, even when it's illogical to do so. You, on the other hand, now know the difference. It's a mistake that's easy to correct, unlike a forgotten backup. Fixing that isn't always possible. Sigh.

Writing Tip #25: "Baited" vs. "Bated"

The only ones who should have "baited breath" are gullible fish or customers of less-than-fresh sushi joints.

- "Bated" means in great suspense.
- "Baited" refers to a lure ready for use.

Make sure you know the difference. You'd rather be fishing? Great. Just don't eat the chum.

Writing Tip #26: "Bear" vs. "Bare"

I know certain toddlers like to "grin and bare it," but that's a bit different, I suppose. The expression most people are looking for is "grin and bear it"—"bear" spelled like the animal, not "bare" like a naked, giggling child.

In conclusion:

- "Bear," when acting as a noun is a woodland creature (Yogi, Fozzie, Smokey . . .).
- "Bear," when acting as a verb, is to hold up under pressure (grin and bear it), to support (to bear a load of bricks), or to produce/bring forth (to bear fruit or to bear a child).
- "Bare," when acting as an adjective or verb, is to be unconcealed, naked, or sparse.

Although I'm all for confidence, people, let's try to keep the grinning and baring it to a minimum. Okay?

Writing Tip #27: "Berth" vs. "Birth"

If you want to give someone a wide berth, that might make sense, but if you're talking about a wide birth, I wonder if you're being a bit more personal than you intended.

"Berth" is a rare word these days for those of us who don't spend much time on seafaring vessels, but it is a word worth spelling correctly when it's called upon.

- A "berth" (noun) commonly means either a place for a ship to dock, a careful distance away from something, or a shelf-like sleeping space one sometimes comes across while traveling.
- To "berth" (verb) usually means to dock a ship.

- The idiom "to give a wide berth" means to give some space to or to keep your distance from.
- A "birth" (noun) is the act of being born. It usually references people, but can also refer to abstracts such as ideas. "Birth" can also refer to lineage or heritage.
- To "birth" (verb) means to give life to, in one way or another. I'll avoid the technicalities that might fascinate or disgust you.
- A "birthday" refers to the day on which one is born. Some fun-loving souls may also refer to their birth-week or birth-month. Depending on how hard they are partying, you might want to give them a wide berth.

That's roughly it when it comes to this pair. I hope that settles it for you.

Writing Tip #28: "Beside" vs. "Besides"

I'm beside myself with frustration about confused usage of "besides" and "beside," but the funny thing is that if I lived long, long ago, this wouldn't be an issue at all. Although "beside" came first, originally in a two-word Old English form, *bī sīdan*, meaning "by the side of," it took its present form by roughly 1200. Of course, at this time, it could be used either as an adverb or as a preposition, and when "besides" became common by 1400, these two forms were used interchangeably. Only in later years did their meanings begin to become distinct.

Lucky for those of you who make this mistake and dream of time travel, set your flux capacitor for 1400, and you'll be all set. For the rest of us:

- "Beside" means to be in a position next to something.
- "Besides" means in addition.

As for being "beside myself," the Middle English definition of "beside" as "outside" is the origin of this expression, meaning to be outside of oneself, practically an out-of-body experience due to some strong emotion. Is that hyperbolic? Absolutely. But those are often the best etymology stories, aren't they?

Writing Tip #29: "Between" vs. "Among"

At first glance, there's a simple distinction between "between" and "among," but the problem is that the age-old adage about "between" being used for a group of two and "among" being used for a larger group isn't actually true. This supposed "rule" harkens back to the original form of "between," *betwēonum*, which meant "by two." However, this was back in the days of Old English, and as we well know, language evolves.

Today, clever writers can remember that the word "between" is always used when referring to specific relationships, in pairs of two or sometimes even more. "Among" is used when the grouping is vague or generalized. Thus:

- We're discussing differences between "between" and "among." (Correct. There are two specific concepts named.)
- There needs be agreement between Silas, Enzo, and Paulo on this topic. (Correct. These are three specific people.)
- There needs to be agreement among writerly folk on this topic. (Correct. "Writerly folk" is generalized; no specific names are named.)
- They are among the words that are most often confused. (Correct. "Words" is generalized.)

Once you understand these differences, maybe you're feeling accomplished and on top of your grammar game. Hold onto that confidence, because the differences go a bit further. The good news is I'm guessing you already know this next piece.

When referring to location, "among" and "between" have more clear-cut differences. For example, "the letter was between the books" is different from "the letter was among the books." In the first sentence, the letter has a book on both sides of it, and in the second, the letter was in the same place as other books.

Thus, concerning location:

- "Between" means in the middle of.
- "Among" means with or in the same location.

Admittedly, there are other usages of "between" and "among," but the ones discussed here are the most commonly confused. Now that you're an expert, I'm sure you'll never have issues with this pair again.

Writing Tip #30: "Born" vs. "Borne"

Sure, you weren't born yesterday, but the differences between "born" and "borne" are admittedly a bit confusing. Why do these two words that are so close to each other even exist? One would do fine, but here we are with the English language keeping us on our toes again.

What many people don't realize is that both of these words are forms of the past participle of "bear," as in to bear children or to bear something heavy on your heart.

- "Born" always refers to a birth, be it literal or metaphorical (for example, born in 1978; a star is born; American-born); however, you have to pay attention to who is giving birth and who is the result of that birth. There's more on that in a moment.
- "Borne" refers to all the other definitions of bear, including carrying, suffering, supporting, or transmitting (for grief to be borne or food-borne illnesses); however, here's the tricky part: it also can relate to birth if it refers to the

one giving birth (for example, his grandmother has borne eight kids; they were borne by her).

Admittedly, the usage of "borne" referring to birth is rarer, but it's worth knowing.

If you are someone who always uses the "born" form, make sure you think about it in the future. Maybe you're always using it correctly, but "born" versus "borne" deserves some consideration.

Writing Tip #31: "Breach" vs. "Breech"

One of these words has to do with breaking, and one of these words has to do with britches and back-ends. Do you know the difference between "breach" and "breech"? Remember:

- "Breach" means the breakage of a law or rule, a gap in a wall or other barrier made most commonly from an act of destruction, a leap, or drastic change in position such as a whale jumping from the water.
- "Breech" means the hind end of the body or the back end of a gun. In its plural form ("breeches"), it can refer to short pants.

The difference of a vowel can make a big difference. In a military command, for example, you might want to breach the enemy lines. You probably don't want to breech the enemy lines. I'm not quite sure what the latter would mean—whether it would be mooning them, pulling down their trousers, or something else—but whatever it is, I don't think the higher authorities would approve.

Writing Tip #32: "Broach" vs. "Brooch"

Brooches might not be the height of fashion these days, but at least their spelling should be. Yes, it's true that "brooch" is pronounced like "coach," but it isn't spelled the same way.

- A "brooch" is a type of jewelry attached to clothing near the neckline by a pin.
- "Broach" is most commonly a verb meaning to mention a topic for the first time (to broach the subject), but it also means to pierce or tap (to broach a keg).

The spelling of "brooch" seems to be a matter of debate for centuries, but dictionaries now agree on the standard spelling. "Broach" is a common typo that has been accepted as an alternate spelling of the jewelry piece in a few rare dictionaries, but I recommend staying safe and using the standard form. It's been used at least as far back as Chaucer, after all. "Send hire letters, tokens, brooches, and rynges," the famous British author wrote in his poem "The Legend of Good Women" in 1385.

I don't feel like I'm broaching a sensitive conversation when discussing "broach" and "brooch"; rather, it seems more a matter of ignorance. There's the rare dictionary that might let you get away with a mistake on these two, but I have faith you can get it right.

Writing Tip #33: "But" vs. "Yet"

As conjunctions, those little words that can connect words, phrases, or sentences, "but" and "yet" are interchangeable. Confusion often falls when they are used in other ways, though, so let's take a moment to discuss these short but sweet terms.

- As an adverb, "but" usually means only (for example, "These words are but one of the examples of differences in definitions between parts of speech.").
- As an adverb, "yet" usually means still, now, or thus far ("Have you figured it out yet?" or "If you haven't yet, keep trying.").

Do you see how "but" and "yet" are no longer interchangeable in these forms? It's a difference worth noting.

Writing Tip #33.1

Avoid using "but yet" together. There is no higher level of contradiction when they are used as a pair. Instead, there's simply a level of wordiness and redundancy.

But Shakespeare used "but yet" often, you say? Indeed he did. He was also striving to write in iambic pentameter. If this is your reasoning as well, I'm okay with this redundancy, but my guess is that's not your style.

Writing Tip #34: "Can" vs. "May"

"Mother, May I?" is so much more than a game. It's a lesson in respect and grammar, isn't it? The game isn't called "Mother, Can I?" (You know where I'm going with this.)

I feel like most people know when we should use "may" and when we should use "can," but no one takes the time to get it right. "May" is all about permission. "Can" is about physical ability.

Example 1: "Can I go to the bathroom?" (I sure hope you can.)

Example 2: "Can I walk down the street?" (It's possible, but it might not be happening.)

Example 3: "May I take three giant steps forward?" (Yes, you may.)

We're all sloppy on this one, so I present a challenge to all of us. Channel the 2nd grade teacher who first introduced you to this rule.

Imagine the look on her face every time a student used these words incorrectly. Take that look to heart. Embrace it. Internalize it. Then do the grammarians in the world (and yourself) a favor, and say it right.

Challenge accepted?

Writing Tip #35: "Capital" vs. "Capitol"

Let's talk about the difference between "capital" and "capitol." It's not a typo, though many non-Americans might assume it's just that. "Capitol" with an "o" refers to the government building in Washington, D.C. or to the building or buildings of a state government. "Capital" with an "a" is every other definition of the word.

Example: I am thankful for those who invested the capital (money) in the capital (excellent) restaurant near the Capitol (building) in the capital (home of state government) of Virginia.

Got it?

Writing Tip #36: "Cite" vs. "Site" vs. "Sight"

"What a sight!" you might say when you see the construction site of the new skyscraper stretching upward toward the clouds. Perhaps you'll take some pictures of it to put up on your website, where you'll cite an interview with the architect.

However you use these words, remember to take a moment to consider which one you actually need for any given instance.

- "Cite" is a verb meaning to pay a source its due. If your words or your research come from somewhere besides your own head, you should cite where you heard such a thing. To "cite" in many ways is to give an official shout-out.
- A "site" is a location. These days, "site" is also used as a common abbreviation for "website."

- "Sight" is one's ability to see. There is eyesight, hindsight, foresight, and second sight, but each of these harkens back to the original definition in one way or another.

For the love of the English language, just like "nite" is not a correct abbreviation of "night," "site" is not an acceptable abbreviation of "sight." Can you please pinkie swear you won't get that one wrong again? Thank you.

Writing Tip #37: "Coarse" vs. "Course"

If you were into woodworking, maybe you'd take a course on coarse woods. If you were a runner, your blood might course through your veins as you got ready to start on the course. If you were being a bit lackadaisical with your punctuation marks, a copyeditor might call you coarse. Oh, the options are almost endless with this pairing.

Remember:

- "Coarse" means rough or made up of large pieces or a loose grain. It can also mean vulgar or rude.
- "Course" means either a series of classes or a path, when it's acting as a noun. As a verb, it means to run or travel quickly.

These two words are often mistaken for each other, but another humorous typo is the misuse of "curse." Although curses can be coarse, please don't let them course through your writing.

I think that just about covers it.

Writing Tip #38: "Compel" vs. "Impel"

What compels you to wake up every morning? It's a good question to ask, whether you're thinking about word choice or not. I hope your

motivation to start out your day, swinging both feet out of your bed, is
something that makes you happy, or if not, I hope it's something that
someday will bring you happiness.

You know what brings me happiness? The correct use of language.
It might not be the sole passion of my existence, but it's definitely something that can bring a smile to my lips. Writing doesn't impel me out of
my bed. It sometimes propels me. It certainly doesn't repel me. But before
we go any further, let's make sure we have these definitions straight:

- "Compel" means to force or drive something along (often
  an action). There is no choice in the matter when you are
  compelled to do something. For example, "The storm
  compelled the tree branch to break" or "The bad guy compelled the hostage to his knees." Note: there's no alternative to this influence.
- "Impel" means to drive something forward, but the drive
  is not forced. There is still a degree of choice in the matter. For example, "The storm impelled me to close my car
  windows" or "The tone of his voice impelled her to speak."
  Note: nothing is involuntary in these usages.

Both of these words find their origins in the Latin word *pellere*, meaning "to drive." "Propel," "repel," "expel," and "dispel" have the same
root.

Is this background compelling? Maybe. Maybe not. Will it compel
you to get these words correct in the future? No. Will it impel you?
Hopefully so.

Writing Tip #39: "Compliment" vs. "Complement"

I would like to give a compliment to you. Perhaps it's your fabulous
grammar know-how. Perhaps it's your bravery to tackle the sometimes

nonsensical English language head-on. Perhaps it's your awesome smartwatch that projects holographics. (Where did you get it? Can I borrow it sometime?)

Whatever the reason, remember my first sentence: "I would like to give a compliment to you."

- If you are looking for the word meaning an expression of praise or admiration, you're looking for a word with an "i" in it: compliment.
- If you are looking for the word meaning something that completes, balances, or pairs well with something else, you're looking for the form with an "e": complement.

If I complimented you on your smartwatch, I could note it complements your new hoverboard, or perhaps the sparkle of sun. Either way, you get the idea.

Writing Tip #40: "Compose" vs. "Comprise"

There are 250 writing tips that compose this book. My book comprises 250 writing tips. There's a subtle difference between these words that is essential in mastering their usage. Are you getting them right?

Ignoring other meanings for a moment, let's focus on when "compose" means to come together to form something. Thus, little pieces come together to make something big. Words compose a page; planets compose the solar system; trees compose a forest.

To "comprise" means to contain, so to use it properly, something big must contain smaller parts. The library comprises books; molecules comprise atoms; the "dead poets society" did not comprise dead poets. (Or maybe it did have one. Oh, I just got sad . . . good movie.)

I can hear the gears grinding in your brain, and you're thinking about more than Neil Perry. What about "to be comprised of," you say?

Maybe you've been told to avoid the passive voice, but here's one case where the passive voice should always be avoided. Never use the phrase "to be comprised of." Technically, it's a bit confusing, and it's commonly considered nonstandard if not completely incorrect. Please stop using it.

Are these "compose" and "comprise" rules ones you've been following? Are they rules you've heard before? Whether this is new information or not, it's time to get it right, folks. (And maybe it's time to rewatch *Dead Poets Society*. I love that film.)

Writing Tip #41: "Conscience" vs. "Conscious"

When you think about your conscience, do you think about Jiminy Cricket who helped a newly conscious puppet named Pinocchio? No? Do you think of an angel and devil sitting on your shoulders? None of these concepts of the conscience are scientifically sound, but there is some true science inside your conscience. Maybe a neurologist or psychologist could speak to specifics, but I'm talking about the word "science." It's hiding there within the word "conscience." Even Jiminy Cricket, who always tells the truth, couldn't argue with that.

Remember:

- "Conscience" is one's inner sense of right versus wrong.
- "Conscious," on the other hand, is to be aware of one's surroundings or existence. It can also mean to be paying attention to what one is doing.

We have to be fully conscious when we're writing, don't we? If we're half asleep, mistakes like mixing up these two happen. Perhaps we should say that we should remain conscientious. Does that confuse things?

Writing Tip #41.1

"Conscientious," which is clearly related to "conscience," means to be attentive, responsible, and meticulous.

Writing Tip #42: "Continual" vs. "Continuous"

Both "continual" and "continuous" stem from the same root as the word "continue," yet there is a subtle difference that is important to know for their correct usage—a difference that brings to mind a similar contrast between "recur" and "reoccur."

- "Continual" means for something to happen repeatedly, but with pauses or interludes between occurrences.
- "Continuous" means for something to continue without interruption.

Typos on social media accounts are continual. If they were continuous, I think I'd give up on digital interaction altogether. On the east coast of the United States, spring showers are continual. If they were continuous, spring would no longer be my favorite season.

The difference between "continual" and "continuous" is subtle, but mastering these subtleties elevates your writing skills to an entirely different level. (See Writing Tip #115: "Recur" vs. "Reoccur" for a similar conversation.)

Writing Tip #43: "Cord" vs. "Chord"

People are cutting the cable cords in their houses a lot these days, and they aren't looking back—except perhaps at their spelling. Did they cut the cord? Or was it the chord? This decision is striking a chord with a generation. Or is it striking a cord?

Have you ever stared at a word so long you over-think it and confuse yourself? As a refresher:

- A "chord" is a musical combination.
- A "cord" is a string or thin rope. It is also a unit of volume used for firewood.
- To "strike a chord," harks back to that music reference, meaning to find something familiar.
- To "cut the cord" means to cut ties with, as in the umbilical cord.

It's funny how our brains leave us at times. That's why this book's here, though—a resource for the moments of temporary bewilderment.

Writing Tip #44: "Convince" vs. "Persuade"

I try to be convincing here—persuasive that grammar is indeed important. Have I convinced you, dear reader? Hopefully. Have I persuaded you? No. Trick question.

Though most people use them interchangeably, "to convince" and "to persuade" should be used in different situations. The difference is all about what someone is being convinced of or persuaded to do.

- You convince someone of an idea.
- You persuade someone to take some sort of action.

Example 1: I want to convince you that word choice matters.
Example 2: Readers of my blog persuaded me to write this book.
Do you see the difference?
And for those of you ready to call out my first sentence, calm yourselves down. The adjective forms of these words are indeed synonyms. (You've got to love the English language.)

Writing Tip #45: "Could Of," "Would Of," and "Should Of" vs. "Could Have," "Would Have," and "Should Have"

Though we're often sloppy in speech, remember that the correct form of these phrases is "could have," "should have," and "would have"—not "could of," "would of," or "should of" and definitely not "coulda," "woulda," and "shoulda."

Example 1: All he should of eaten is one slice of pumpkin pie. (Incorrect.)

Example 2: If he stopped at one slice, his pants would have still fit. (Correct.)

Nonstandard usage in conversation is fine; in writing, it simply makes you look silly.

Writing Tip #46: "Council" vs. "Counsel"

One is a noun, and one is a verb. I'll give you a moment to think about that. Got it? Okay, let's see if you have it right.

- A "council" (noun) is a group of people providing advice or establishing rules and laws.
- To "counsel" (verb) is to give advice.

Making sure we're covering our bases,

- A "counselor" is a person whose job is to provide advice. It can also be a person whose job is to help kids at summer camp, but there's advice being departed along the way in those cases as well.
- A "counsellor" is the exact same person in a place outside of the United States.

Oh there we Americans go, being rebels again. Other slight variations that should be noted include "counseled" vs. "counselled" and
"counseling" vs. "counselling." Why Americans and Americans alone
prefer the single L probably has some reasoning behind it—at least
you'd think so—but I have yet to discover it.

Should you go to the consulate and visit the consul about this?
Probably not. That might add to the confusion.

Writing Tip #47: "Defuse" vs. "Diffuse"

You've got to love confusing homonyms—or perhaps near-homonyms
in this case. So often we know what we mean, but then we spell the
first thing that comes to our mind. Spell-check doesn't help in these
cases, does it? Maybe Microsoft has someone working on that. Or
maybe there's hope in Google or Apple.

Either way, until a tech giant saves the spelling-impaired, here are
some simple reminders:

- "Defuse" means to make less dangerous, tense, or awk-
  ward. Its simplest use concerns the removal of a fuse—as
  in a bomb. With a pocket knife and duct tape. While
  doing work for the Phoenix Foundation. (Okay, perhaps
  the *MacGyver* piece is unnecessary for the exact definition, but you get the idea.)
- "Diffuse," on the other hand, means to spread out or scat-
  ter. For the physics buffs out there, its simplest definition
  is "to spread by diffusion." For those of us to whom this
  means nothing, think about "diffused light"—sunlight
  breaking through the morning fog as it lifts off the
  river . . . illuminating a chase of one of Murdock's lackeys
  by a spy who's rigged up an explosion downstream with a
  shoelace, a pocket watch, and a potato. (Too much?)

Writing Tip #48: "Discreet" vs. "Discrete"

I'll be discreet when I tell you that a long time ago these two words had the same etymological origin, but that they have become discrete with time. How does one stay discreet when discussing the roots of language? A hand over the mouth? A subtle lean in? Do I send it via text message?

- "Discrete" means to be separated or distinct, like the two "E"s within this word. The "E"s are discrete within "discrete."
- "Discreet," on the other hand, means to be cautious, reserved, or unobtrusive, especially in speech.

What fascinates me about the origin of language is that the logical sometimes becomes nonsensical and the nonsensical somehow becomes logical. This is the story of these two words.

Long ago, when they were baby words, they were born from the Latin *discrētus*, which meant both "to separate" and "to differentiate." When they first crawled into the English language in the fourteenth century, they didn't quite have a grasp on standard spelling; thus, this single word was sometimes spelled "discret," sometimes "discrete," and sometimes "discreet." Childhood was a playful time, where "discreet" reigned supreme and childish alternative nicknames were temporarily forgotten, but then by the sixteenth century, moody adolescence struck and its spelling again became fickle, shifting between "discrete," "discreet," "dyscrete," and "discreete," like a teenager trying on personas.

Today, though, these two words have come into adulthood and come to terms with their individual identities. And it's time for the writers among us to come to terms with them too.

Writing Tip #49: "Disinterested" vs. "Uninterested"

"Disinterested" and "uninterested" actually have different meanings. Yep, this is me calling you out again.

- To be "disinterested" means to be impartial. A disinterested person wouldn't have a stake in the outcome.
- To be "uninterested" means that you simply don't care.

This is a subtle difference, but one worth noting.
Example 1: A disinterested referee would call the game fairly.
Example 2: An uninterested referee might not be paying much attention.

There are some words that people use as synonyms when they really aren't. Have you been using these words correctly?

Writing Tip #50: "Dived" vs. "Dove"

What flows more naturally to your ear, "She dived into the water" or "She dove into the water"? One of these constructions has been correct since roughly 1300, and the other was first misused about two centuries ago. Do you know the difference? And more importantly, does it even matter?

- "Dived" was the original past form of the word "dive," and to many (largely British) audiences, it still holds the title as the correct form.
- "Dove" came to be in the 1800s, following the past-tense pattern of the verb "drive/drove." Today, "dove" is the more common form in both spoken and written text in the United States and Canada.

But just because it's more common, is it right?

Oh, you know "right" is such a flexible word when it comes to the transition of language. However, it is indeed considered acceptable and preferred to most audiences on this side of the Atlantic. Thus:

- William Shakespeare dived into his work.
- Mark Twain dove into the Mississippi River.

What do you think?

Writing Tip #51: "Doing Good" vs. "Doing Well"

Here's one of my biggest grammatical pet peeves: the use of an adjective when an adverb is correct. Getting back to basics, adjectives modify nouns; adverbs modify verbs, adjectives, or other adverbs.

Example 1:

Q: How are you doing?

A: I'm doing good/great/terrific. (Cringe. Incorrect, though you hear it all the time. These are all adjectives. They cannot modify "doing," a verb.)

A: I'm doing well/fine/fabulously/horrifically. (Woohoo! Correct. These are all adverbs—though I'm sorry about the "horrifically." What can I do to make you feel better?)

Example 2:

Q: How'd the game go?

A: They played bad/awesome. (Incorrect. Again, these are adjectives.)

A: The team played terribly/awesomely/cohesively/like gods. (Correct. These are all adverbs except for the last one, which was a simile. Who's paying attention?)

Okay, I'll get off my grammarian high horse now.

Writing Tip #52: "Due Diligence" vs. "Do Diligence"

If you want to do the right thing, maybe you want to do diligence. The problem is that this doesn't really make any sense.

The correct expression is "due diligence," which has some variations of meanings depending on whether its use is in legal, business, or general writing. In essence, though, "due diligence" means to be comprehensive and thoughtful in the research of something before moving forward. Perhaps this is buying a house. Maybe it's going through a merger. It's possibly even comparing baby food brands when you have a little bundle on the way.

When people discuss "due diligence," many claim that this is a legal term that has found its way into everyday speech somewhere in the past few decades. The secret most don't realize is that this phrase has been used since the mid-fifteenth century, and although it did transform into a legal concept somewhere along the way, it didn't start out this way. Even etymologists need to do their due diligence it seems.

Writing Tip #53: "Dual" vs. "Duel"

Maybe it's just me, but I've seen this one confused a number of times. It leads to some interesting typos. "Duel chamber waterbeds"? Really?

Here's your quick reminder.

- "Dual" refers to something having two parts.
- A "duel" is a fight between two people—think Alexander Hamilton and Aaron Burr.

Not to call out those waterbeds. Maybe this spelling was intentional. Waterbed fight club anyone?

Writing Tip #54: "Each One Worse Than the Next" vs. "Each One Worse Than the Last"

If you have psychic powers and you can see what's coming up next, using the phrase "each one worse than the next" might be okay for you. Otherwise, you should write, "each one worse than the last."

For those who suffer from "coulrophobia," also known as a fear of clowns, a parade of these silly, whimsical, but often creepy characters might not be a fun experience. After a certain number of large painted mouths and red ball noses, it might seem like each one is worse than the last—one on stilts wobbling a bit too close, countless of them climbing out of a tiny car. Fear is intensifying the experience, and it gets worse with every one that passes by.

If that poor soul suffering from coulrophobia was to say, "each one worse than the next," he or she would know for a fact who is around that street corner, but we can't know this. We only know what we've seen.

I know clowns are a drastic example, but I think you see my point.

Did Stephen King's *It* traumatize anyone else?

Writing Tip #55: "Economic" vs. "Economical"

Many schools offer classes in economics, but not many offer classes on how to be economical. The latter could be an independent study for a lifetime, I suppose.

Although these two words clearly have the same root in finance, remember that they are different terms.

- "Economic" is an adjective, meaning having to do with the economy or finances.
- "Economical" is an adjective, meaning to be thrifty, prudent, or wise with one's spending.

An economic strategy can be put into place when discussing the national debt. An economical strategy might include the use of coupons and watching for sales. It's a common mistake to use "economic" for both meanings, but don't forget the additional letters when you need them. Skipping letters isn't economical; it's simply wrong.

Writing Tip #56: "Elicit" vs. "Illicit"

If you wanted just one more game of bingo after a five-hour bingo marathon in North Carolina, you would be eliciting something illicit. (North Carolina's administrative code prohibits games longer than this length.)

If you wanted to take your pet ferret out to see if it could help you hunt in the mountains of West Virginia, you might be eliciting something illicit. (It's illegal in West Virginia to pursue wild birds or other animals with a ferret. If this law is broken, a fee and jail time are in order.)

If you wanted to grease a pig in Minnesota and then challenge friends to catch it, you might be eliciting something illicit. (Both "greasing" and "oiling" pigs is illegal in Minnesota if a catching game is involved.)

I really want to go on, but I won't. Long story short, this is a fun pairing of near homonyms.

Remember:

- "Elicit," a verb, means to extract, draw forth, evoke, or prompt.
- "Illicit," an adjective, means to be forbidden, either by law, rule, or cultural values.

Funny typos arise when one confuses "elicit" vs. "illicit." Don't talk about "elicit drugs," or someone will think you're looking for some.

Don't talk about trying to "illicit a favor," or someone might be a bit worried about your intentions.

Take your time with this pair, making sure you get your spelling right. All right?

Writing Tip #57: "Elusive" vs. "Allusive" vs. "Illusive"

The meanings of these three words might seem elusive, but they are easy to get ahold of if you try. Thinking of related words can help. "Elusive" is related to "elude" and "elusiveness"; "allusive" is related to "allude" and "allusion"; "illusive" is related to "illusion." Of course, if you have a good handle on "allusion" versus "illusion" (see Writing Tip #13), I probably don't even have anything else I need to say.

Just in case, though, remember:

- "Elusive" means difficult to grab or catch, either physically or mentally. A pet hamster might be elusive, but so could the numbers on your gym locker lock.
- "Allusive" means to hint at something rather than to directly refer to it. When comparing your great aunt to a Galapagos tortoise, you aren't saying that she's old. You're being allusive. (Though I still wouldn't recommend it.)
- "Illusive" means to not be based in fact or reality. If you try to catch a rainbow, it might seem elusive, but the rainbow itself is illusive, a visual illusion.

I won't be allusive or beat around the bush when I say that these are words that you need to figure out. They are commonly confused, but what's a little vowel confusion? Don't let those vowels win. This trio can be conquered once and for all.

Writing Tip #58: "Emigrate" vs. "Immigrate"

People often forget that there are two terms to use when discussing moving from one country to another. There's no trick except remembering that immigrating and emigrating are two sides of a conversation.

- "Immigrate" means to come to a new country to live.
- "Emigrate" means to leave one's country to live somewhere else.

One immigrates *to* and emigrates *from*.

There's also "migrate," as in moving from one location or habitat to another, but "migration" doesn't hint of the permanence of "immigrate" or "emigrate."

Immigration is a tricky subject to discuss, but the verb forms around it are less so. It's time to settle this side of the issue once and for all, isn't it?

Writing Tip #59: "Eminent" vs. "Imminent"

If someone was in eminent danger, is this a danger with a certain amount of prestige? When I see this typo, which I sadly have seen far more than once, it makes me giggle a little bit before pulling out my red pen.

Of course, the opposite error occurs perhaps more frequently. Perhaps you want to speak of a high religious official and you refer to him as imminent. I really hope that's not what you meant to say unless we're talking about a high church conspiracy novel of one kind or another.

Remember:

- "Eminent" means prestigious, distinguished, or high in station. The Pope is eminent, for example.

- "Imminent" means impending or threatening, something that could happen at any moment. A hurricane's arrival might be imminent.

I do still wonder about that eminent danger, though. There's a story there. Who's going to write it?

Writing Tip #60: "Everyday" vs. "Every Day"

We are only human. We sin every day. Or maybe I should reword that. "Sin" might be a bit strong. Perhaps I should say that we mistype "everyday" nearly every day.

Do you know the difference between when it should be one word versus two?

Some rules are hard to remember, but this one shouldn't be.

- "Everyday" (one word) is simply an adjective, meaning commonplace, informal, or normal.
- "Every day" (two words) is a time expression, meaning "each day."

I might have started off this tip a little severe. No one's going anywhere hot and fiery for confusing these two words. But getting language right is a little bit of heaven, no?

Writing Tip #61: "Explicit" vs. "Implicit"

Knowing the difference between "implicit" and "explicit" is knowing the difference between "implying" and "explaining."

- If something is said directly, the speaker is being explicit.
- If something is being said between the lines, the speaker is being implicit.

I remember buying my first CD that had a "Parental Advisory: Explicit Lyrics" sticker on it. I felt like such a rebel with my new Alanis Morissette album in my hands. If it had been "implicit lyrics," there wouldn't have been any warnings. "Implicit lyrics" are all over the place.

Writing Tip #62: "Famous" vs. "Notorious"

What pops into your head when you hear the word "notorious"? Duran Duran? The Notorious B.I.G.? Sure these are famous musical artists, but don't let this mislead you into believing the biggest confusion around this word:

"Notorious" is not a synonym of famous.

Yes, "notorious" shares the same Latin root (*nōscere*) as "noteworthy" and "notable," but as far back as at least 1549 when it was used in *The Book of Common Prayer*, "notorious" has meant well-known for bad reasons. You cannot forget the second half of the definition. We should not aspire to be notorious any more than we should aspire to be infamous. (Hint: "infamous" is not the same as "famous.")

Whatever song or image the word brings to your mind, make sure you fully understand "notorious" before you use it in your writing or conversations.

Writing Tip #63: "Farther" vs. "Further"

Do you know the difference between "further" and "farther"? Did you realize that these are indeed two different words? No?

- Only use "farther" when talking about measurable distance. You can run farther, drive farther, see farther, and so on.

- "Further" comes into play when something additional is needed. Someone might need further information, further depth, further growth, and so on.

If you need "farther" details, I suppose I suggest running to get there faster. Is that helpful?

Writing Tip #64: "Fawn" vs. "Faun"

Young children are often drawn to baby animals, and who really blames them? There are not many things more precious than a baby bunny or a soft little lamb or a wrinkle-nosed hedgehog. (Yes, a baby hedgehog—if you haven't seen one, you can't argue.) Some little ones probably even fawn over fawn-colored fawns; however, note that a "faun" is a different creature altogether.

- As a noun, a "fawn" is a baby caribou, pronghorn, or deer.
- As an adjective, "fawn" is a light brownish-yellow color.
- As a verb, "fawn" means to dote upon or to act in a servile position in order to gain favor.
- "Faun" is a noun meaning a mythological deity of the countryside, most commonly with the legs, backside, horns, and ears of a goat.

Maybe a faun is playing a reed pipe and dancing with Pan; maybe a faun is a resident of Narnia that is quick to protect children who travel there through wardrobes; maybe a faun is helping Puck cause mischief with magical love potions. But chances are that a faun isn't a friend of Bambi's.

Writing Tip #65: "Female" vs. "Woman"

Reporters at sporting events often have questionable use of feminine descriptors. I'm not even talking about the difference in "Women's Hockey" versus "Ladies' Figure Skating" or the use of "girls" when commentators wouldn't dream of calling male athletes "boys." Those are semantic conversations unto themselves, and this isn't the place for them. I'm talking about the use of "women" as an adjective. (Pssst . . . hey, writers. "Women" is a noun!)

When you're looking for the adjective form of "women," "female" is usually your best bet; however, time and time again, writers are using the wrong part of speech.

It's everywhere: "women athletes," "woman astronaut," "woman candidate," and so many more. I could go on, but I won't. I could have a bigger conversation I really want to have, but I won't.

When you look up the word "woman" in the dictionary, you'll see it marked as a noun—only a noun. What do rules matter, you say? Well, in my humble opinion, they matter a lot.

Writing Tip #66: "Fictional" vs. "Fictitious"

If a pathological liar tells stories, are they fictional or fictitious? If those stories are then published, does the word choice need to change?

Here's a subtle one for you. Both "fictional" and "fictitious" share a common root, but there is a difference in their definitions.

- "Fiction," of course, is imaginary or fabricated.
- Something is described as "fictional" when it relates to a work of art, such as a book, a film, or a painting.
- When something is fabricated in real life (à la "Liar, liar, pants on fire"), it is considered "fictitious."

My question concerns Pinocchio's nose. Is the nose fictional, but it grows when he tells something fictitious? It's a linguistic mystery of the universe, my friends.

Writing Tip #67: Don't "Feel Badly"

Do you have the inability to feel? If so, you feel badly. If you're talking about your state of mind, you feel bad.

Let's take a moment to discuss sensory verbs, such as feel, taste, smell, sound, and look. As a gentle reminder, if you need a word to modify a noun, use an adjective. If you are modifying a verb, use an adverb. I know this gets tricky when the modifier is next to the verb—not the noun—but take a moment to consider it before jotting it down. For some reason, when it comes to sensory verbs, people seem to trip up.

Example 1: "James Brown feels good." "Good" is an adjective, modifying James Brown. If James Brown was having a rough day, he'd feel bad. If he felt "badly," he would either be bad at empathizing or have some sort of sensory condition worth discussing with a doctor.

Example 2: "Dinner tasted delicious," would be correct. If dinner tasted "deliciously," I'd have all sorts of other questions about the live thing you were eating and then what perhaps it was eating.

It's all about those 3rd grade basics: what adjectives and adverbs modify. I know we all make mistakes on occasion, but try hard to get this one right.

Writing Tip #68: "Few" vs. "Less"

In live election-coverage, one mistake is made over and over again. I'm talking about vote counts. Oh yes, I'm going there. Social faux-pas be darned.

This is important, folks. Let's talk about the difference between "less" and "fewer." (What? You thought I was going in a different direction?) The most common explanation of these two words is that:

- "Less" is properly used in a comparison when the different amounts in question are not countable (for example, less happy, less powerful, less rice, less sand on the beach).
- "Fewer" is properly used in a comparison when the different amounts are countable (for example, fewer votes, fewer people, fewer apples, fewer boxes of cereal).

However, sadly for those who have used these guidelines as their rule of thumb for years, it is a few degrees more complicated than that. The "countable" rule is one of relatively newer construction, and it's not one that all language authorities agree upon.

Thus, here's the guideline I recommend following:

- Use "fewer" when the items in question are plural. For example, fewer bowling pins were left standing; she had fewer dreams last night than the night before; there were fewer digits on his paycheck than he would have liked.
- Use "less" when the item in question is singular or doesn't have a plural. For example, he knocked down one less bowling pin than she did; she got less sleep than the night before; there was less money in his paycheck than he expected.

Do you see how in that last example, you could argue that money is countable, as are bowling pins? But in the "less" examples, the words in the sentence are singular, thus "less" is correct.

Is this the clear cut end of the story? Maybe, maybe not. For some concepts, such as precise measurements, times, weights, and amounts of money, writers need to take extra consideration.

Sure, 26 miles is a long distance for a race, but do you note how I used the singular verb "is" to describe it? The same construction follows for other ideas in these categories. Three hundred fifty-six days is a long time to wait until your next birthday. Five pounds of produce is sometimes hard to juggle. One billion dollars is a lot of money. In our minds, these subjects can seem plural; however, in our sentence construction we give them a singular verb without a second thought. These collections are understood as a singular mass or grouping, whether we would initially think of them that way or not.

Remember the singular versus plural rule, and you'll be well on your way. If you can also remember to give a second glance to measurement, time, weight, and money concepts, you'll be golden.

But in the end, I'll return to all of those declarations of candidates winning less votes. No matter what guideline you follow, that is simply wrong. And when a news outlet's grammar is questionable, they've already lost my faith.

These are the subtleties that sometimes are never taught, but now that you know, it's time to get it right.

Writing Tip #69: "Flaunt" vs. "Flout"

When grandma yells, "You'll never get me, copper!" out her car window as she speeds by, she's flouting the law. Maybe she's doing it by flaunting her new little red corvette. This doesn't sound like your grandmother, you say? Who knows? Maybe she has a wild side waiting to break out.

The difference in these words is not a matter of pronunciation. It's a matter of there being two different words.

- "Flaunt" means to show off or to display proudly.
- "Flout" means to show contempt for.

Don't flout the rules of the English language by flaunting your bad word choice. I promise you, no one will be impressed.

Writing Tip #70: "Fortuitous" vs. "Fortunate"

Are you aware that both "fortuitous" and "fortunate" don't necessarily imply any degree of luck?

Yes, to be "fortunate" is to be lucky or auspicious. For something to be "fortuitous," however, it means that it happened by chance or by accident. There is no positive or lucky implication inherent in this latter word.

Of course, the English language is a malleable thing—whether the by-the-book grammarians of the world like it or not. Because of this fortunate/fortuitous confusion, recent dictionaries have started to include a second "informal" definition of "fortuitous" as "something favorable or lucky that happens by chance." Is this the true meaning? No. But like "literally" now can mean the opposite of literally, "fortuitous" can now mean a misunderstood version of its definition. Sigh.

Take it or leave it, but now you can at least be aware you're annoying the grammar-righteous. And knowing you're troubling people is the first step, I suppose.

Writing Tip #71: "Foreword" vs. "Forward"

More writing tips? Forward ho!

Interestingly, "Forward Ho" was the name of a ship that sailed between England and Japan in the late 1800s. Launched in 1867 and wrecked in 1881, now the vessel is nothing more than a footnote in British sailing history.

If there was a book about it, maybe in there would be a foreword about Forward Ho. Did you catch that spelling difference? Let's be careful with these two words, because they are indeed two different words.

- "Forward" has many definitions, from an adverb meaning ahead or toward the front, to an adjective meaning presumptuous or bold, to a noun referring to a soccer or basketball player's position.
- A "foreword" is a short introduction or opening statement in a published work, and it is generally written by someone other than the author.

Whether you're moving forward full steam ahead, writing a book about nautical history, running out onto the soccer field, or otherwise, make sure you are using the proper term.

Here's a hint for the writing crowd pursuing publication: are you looking for a way to have a book proposal rejected? Often, including a "forward" in your table of contents is enough.

Writing Tip #72: "Gambit" vs. "Gamut"

A musical medieval monk gets the credit for one of these words, and the other has its earliest English origins tied to the game of chess. Any guesses which is which?

While that's percolating in the back of your mind, I'll ask another question: is the expression "runs the gamut" or "runs the gambit"? Or is it "runs the gauntlet"? I ask because this is the idiom where confusion between these two (sometimes three) words occurs most often.

Remember:

- A "gambit" is a calculated move where one seeks to gain the advantage.
- A "gamut" is a whole series or the full range of something.

Did you make your guesses about the monk? His name was Guido d'Arezzo, and in the eleventh century, he developed a new musical scale, using the terms *gamma* and *ut* to denote the first line of his bass staff and the first note, respectively. In time, his *gamma* and *ut* were shortened into "gamut," and it no longer only meant the first note of the first staff. "Gamut" became used to represent the entire scale. That's why it represents a full range or spectrum today, as it has since 1626.

Chess players, on the other hand, know all about gambits, originally coming from the Italian *gambetto*. Sometimes it's worth it to lose one lesser piece for the greater good of the game. Outside of chess, the media reports on gambits in politics all of the time.

Lastly, the correct expression is "runs the gamut," as in covers the full spectrum.

How'd you do with your answers?

Writing Tip #72.1

A "gauntlet" is a glove-like hand covering worn with a suit of armor. This word is most commonly used today in the expression to "throw down the gauntlet," meaning to pose a personal, physical challenge. There aren't many of us who have literal gauntlets lying around.

Writing Tip #73: "Grisly" vs. "Grizzly"

When it's springtime, it's a time for frolicking amidst fields of flowers, listening to the singing birds, and walking in the woods surrounded by the smells of fresh air and newly budding branches. It's also a time to watch out for groggy bears coming out of hibernation.

A tip:

- "Grisly" means gruesome or revolting.
- "Grizzly" is a type of bear.

What you do when you see one, I really don't know, but don't insult the animal by calling it hideous. You don't look so hot when you wake up either.

Writing Tip #74: "Hear" vs. "Here"

"Hear, hear!" you might hear shouted upon a public reading of these writing tips. At least, in my head, that's what happens. This exclamation is an old-fashioned encouragement, the equivalent of a good "Amen" in other circles. It was derived from a common expression of the English Parliament in the late seventeenth century, "Hear him! Hear him!" It doesn't have any connection to "Here! Here!" which is what you might say if you're playing pick-up basketball and you want someone to throw you the ball.

British Parliamentary and sporting calls aside, remember the basics with this pair:

- "Hear" has to do with "hearing" and the ears.
- "Here" has to do with a specific place or location.

The confusion between these two words might simply be a matter of not proofing yourself before you share your communications—whatever they may be—but I, for one, see this mistake far more often than I should. Let's do better.

Do I hear a "Hear, hear"?

Of course, an "Amen" will also do.

Writing Tip #75: "Historic" vs. "Historical"

Although "pre-historic" might cause some confusion to this lesson, remember that:

- "Historic" is an adjective denoting an important event in history.
- "Historical" refers to something in the more distant past.

Perhaps you read "historical romance." This would indeed be different if it was "historic romance"—more Napoleon and Josephine Bonaparte and less unlaced corsets and smelling salts. Though perhaps I need a better example, the French being the French and all.

The invention of the Internet was historic; the cloning of Dolly the sheep was historic; the publication of this book was historic (right? right?). But none of these examples are historical. See the difference? Edit yourselves carefully.

Writing Tip #75.1

"Prehistoric" refers to a period so long ago that there is no written record of the time—before ("pre-") history came to be. While after learning the differences between "historic" and "historical," you might want to extend these differences into the creation of a new, more logical word, "pre-historical," try to hold back. This latter form isn't actually a word.

Writing Tip #76: "Horde" vs. "Hoard"

Think fast. How do you spell the name of the television show where people have collected (or refused to throw away) mountains upon mountains of stuff?

Answer: The show's name is *Hoarders*.

The decision of using "horde" vs. "hoard" often isn't a matter of thought; rather, it's a matter of whatever spills out onto one's keyboard, but that ends here. It's time to pick up after ourselves and put everything in its proper place—including our vowels in these two words.

Remember:

- "Horde" is a noun, which means a crowd, and it's usually used with a negative connotation (for example, a horde of angry shoppers on Black Friday).
- "Hoard" can be a noun, meaning a collection of something amassed for later use, or a verb, meaning the act of collecting and storing the aforementioned belongings.

Yes, they sound the same, but clean up your act, folks. Edit yourselves to get "horde" and "hoard" right.

Writing Tip #77: "i.e." vs. "e.g."

People confuse "i.e." and "e.g." all the time, often not knowing that there's a difference. Breaking it down Julius Caesar style:

- "i.e." is short for "*id est*" or roughly "that is."
- "e.g." is short for "*exempli gratia*" or "for example."

So when you're trying to be at your writerly best (i.e., showing off your grammarian know-how), make sure you don't incur the wrath of those who know the difference (e.g., grammar nazis, disgruntled Latin teachers, or anyone going by the name of Brutus).

Writing Tip #78: "If" vs. "Whether"

In many instances, "if" and "whether" are interchangeable; however—whether we like it or not—this isn't true for all usages. Sure, there's a lot you can get away with in situations where many people won't bat an eye, but then comes the one time you need to get it right: that college essay, that job application, that letter to your boss about your potential promotion . . .

Knowing the rules of the subtleties of the English language can help your cause.

Push up your sleeves, folks. Let's dive into some technicalities.

- Think about your basic "if . . . then . . . " sentence. It's all about creating a condition. If something happens, then something else will happen (e.g., if you add a spoonful of sugar, then the medicine will, in theory, go down). It is always a matter of a singular condition (e.g., let me know if you want to watch *Mary Poppins* later).
- "Whether" is all about options. For instance, "I don't know whether I will watch *Mary Poppins* or *The Sound of Music*" or "Whether I'm singing or not, I kind of want to twirl around with arms outspread atop mountains."

There are a lot of rules about using "whether" after prepositions (for example, I'm thinking about whether Julie Andrews is really good with children) and before a "to-infinitives" (I don't know whether to sing, dance, or frolic), but I think an English-speaking ear can already tell you all of these things.

Some argue that using "whether" instead of "if" in some acceptable interchangeable instances adds a degree of formality. There may be something to this point, but I don't think it's anything to stress over.

Phew. Feel like you have a handle on it? Remember, it's conditions versus options. Beyond that, in my opinion, trust your gut. Guts are often right. Especially when they're filled with a spoonful of sugar, I hear.

Writing Tip #79: "Imply" vs. "Infer"

Implying and inferring often dance together. They might be hand in hand or cheek to cheek, but though they can be partners, they are each looking in different directions. One talks, and the other listens. One has beliefs she wants to subtly express, and one tries to make up her own mind.

- To "imply" means to hint at or suggest without stating anything directly. In Writing Tip #61, we discussed "implicit" vs. "explicit" if you want to bask in the glory of further discussion of this idea.
- To "infer" means to come to a conclusion from hearing reasoning and research. It does not mean understanding something that is directly stated.

Although "infer" is perhaps not the most commonly used of words, there's no reason for confusion with this pair. Yes, they both start with the letter "i," and they both are five letters. That shouldn't be enough to convince you that they are the same. Think of them dancing together—one implies, and one infers—and then you can remember the difference.

Writing Tip #80: "Inquire" vs. "Enquire"

Inquiring minds want to know: is there a difference between "inquire" and "enquire"? What about a difference in "inquiry" and "enquiry"? Which one flows off of your tongue, or should I say, which one flows off of your fingers and onto your keyboard?

If you're looking for a subtle distinction, there is one (ooh, a teaser . . .), but in almost all cases, the words are interchangeable. The biggest difference is that "inquire" and "inquiry" are more common in American English, whereas "enquire" and "enquiry" are more common in British English.

To some across the pond, "to enquire" means to ask more generally, and "to inquire" implies a formal investigation; however, if you're Stateside, I wouldn't really worry about this. Stick to "inquire" and "inquiry" for all uses, and you'll be fine.

Writing Tip #81: "Instill" vs. "Install"

If your grandmother installed certain values in you, I have to ask, are you an android of some sort? Was your kindness downloaded? Was your generosity transferred via a floppy disk? Do you see the difference a single letter can make?

- To "instill" means to establish something in one's mind through time. You instill feelings, ideas, or attitudes.
- To "install" means to put in position (physically or digitally) ready for use. You install programs, equipment, or machinery.

Catching an "instill" vs. "install" typo always makes me want to ask probing questions. But I won't. I'll hold back. At least, I'll try really, really hard to.

Beep. Beep. Boop. Happy writing.

Writing Tip #82: "Insure" vs. "Ensure"

When it's hurricane season, I'm always happy I don't live too close to the coast—though we've had some crazy hurricanes in recent years, so who knows what will happen next. How insured am I in case of a hurricane? How could I ensure the safety of my loved ones? Do you see where I'm going with this one? "Insure" and "ensure" cause nearly as much upset as a tropical storm moving into a patch of warm water. Almost.

Remember:

- "Insure" deals exclusively with the offering of insurance.
- To "ensure" means to make sure, to make safe, or to guarantee.

It's a simple clarification really, but one that somehow still befuddles.

So this hurricane season, insure your properties and ensure your outdoor tables and chairs won't blow away. Assure your family that they don't need to worry while you're at it. Who knows what the weather will bring, but at least your grammar won't be unruly.

Writing Tip #83: "Into" vs. "In to"

People overdo "into" all of the time. Sometimes "in" and "to" are just friendly neighbors who happen to coexist in a simple platonic relationship.

- "Into" is a preposition most often answering a "where" question. Where did I put my wallet? Into my pocket. Where did you get that camo? When I went into an intense kickball league.
- "In to," on the other hand, are two words in a sentence. He went in to see what happened. She swished it in to win the game.

A simple reminder, if you're unsure whether you need to use "into" or "in to," ask yourself the question, "where?" If your sentence answers that question, you need "into"—the preposition. Otherwise, maybe you happen to be using these two words ("in" and "to") next to each other. Maybe it's a short version of "in order to," or maybe it's not. But if it answers "where," it should be one word.

And yes, the saying "into" as in a hobby ("really into stamp collecting") or a love interest ("really into grammarians") is correctly written as one word.

Writing Tip #84: "It's" vs. "Its"

Apostrophes can befuddle us so easily. (Side note: don't you love the word "befuddle"?)

- It's: a contraction of "it is."
- Its: a possessive pronoun.
- Its': not a word.

I understand the logic of seeing an apostrophe "s" and thinking possessive. I really get it. But the English language is full of exceptions. This is one that we need to dedicate to memory.

Your apostrophe placement (or lack thereof) is important, folks!

Writing Tip #85: "Knelt" vs. "Kneeled"

There are some verbs with a rebellious nature that have two past tense forms. Maybe you can recognize them by their tiny fists thrown up in the air. Sometimes one of these forms is right, and one is clearly wrong. Sometimes one is an archaic spelling that still pops up every once in a while, but should only be used for the sake of nostalgia. Sometimes, a verb's past tense can be defined by national borders. And then there's "knelt" and "kneeled."

This is the story of two correct answers. Both "knelt" and "kneeled" are recognized by most dictionaries as correct. Whichever form rolls off your tongue or your pen-tip, go for it. No one can say you're wrong. Is this annoying or liberating? I can't decide.

Although the word "kneel" has been around for a long time, first appearing in English in the twelfth century, originating in the Old English *cnēowlian*, the past tense form of "knelt" only gained popularity in the nineteenth century. Here, it mirrors the verb form of "feel," which turns into "felt" in the past tense. Personally, I'm blaming the

British Romantic poets for this shift. "Knelt" rings more poetic to my ear than "kneeled," but this is a hunch with little research behind it, so don't quote me on that.

Maybe my ear connects "knelt" with poetry, because "kneeled" is the form most commonly to flow from my mouth, but those British Romantic poets were certainly rebels in their own right. If anyone would ever be in a place to make words throw their little fists in the air, it would be them, and with their literary prowess, the form stuck.

However, I don't mean to sway you in either direction. As I noted, both "knelt" and "kneeled" are fair answers. It's rare to be able to choose the word that fits best for you—no poetic license necessary. Whether you choose a favorite form or change your usage from day to day is up to you.

Writing Tip #86: "Lay" vs. "Lie"

If you've ever told a dog to "lay down," you've been teaching it poor grammar. It makes me wonder if there's ever been a picky editor out there who has taught a dog to bark upon "lay down" and listen obediently only to "lie down." Hmm . . . this is giving me some interesting ideas.

Dog training schemes aside, the difference between "lay" and "lie" is one of those conversations that is quick to intimidate and quick to turn judgmental, but that ends here. It's not as tricky as it seems:

- "Lay" always needs an object. (Oh, I'm seeing your eyes glaze over. Stick with me.) In other words, when you use the word "lay," something is being set down and that something is not the subject of the sentence. For example, "I lay the dog treat down" and "I lay down the law" are both correct.

- "Lie," on the other hand, should be used when the action is being done by the subject. I lie down. The dog lies down. If the grammar is making you woozy, you should lie down.

  See the difference?

There doesn't need to be any grammarian snobbery about this pair. Only dog training snobbery. I think I'd be okay with that.

Writing Tip #87: "Lay" vs. "Laid"

Of course, you know that one lies down (the subject taking the action) or one could lay down a rug (the direct object having something done to it)—see Writing Tip #86 for more details—but now, what happens if this laying and lying happened yesterday?

Egads! There's more? Yep, but once you've learned the present tense of this pair, the rest is fairly simple.

- The past tense of "lay" is "laid."
- The past tense of "lie" is "lay."

I know. It's like a grammatical practical joke that "lie" turns into "lay," but there you have it.

Right now, I could lay down my laptop. Yesterday, I laid down my laptop. Right now, I could tell my dog to "lie down." Yesterday, he "lay" down.

Personally, I'm enjoying writing about my pretend dog and the tricks he can do. He can also juggle, have I mentioned that? He juggles and howls to the tune of "Hound Dog." Too much? Maybe it's time for me to lie down.

To finish the past tense puzzle:

- The past participle of "lie" is "lain," as in, "I have lain on the couch for too long."

- The past participle of "lay" is "laid" (just like the past tense), as in, "I had laid it out so clearly."

And now you can conquer "lay" and "lie" in all tenses. Watch out, world!

———————

Writing Tip #88: "Lead" vs. "Led"

Imagine a leader carrying a lead pencil as she led her forces onward. Have the mental image? That's good because I don't think they make lead pencils anymore. I think they're all graphite. At least that's what I've been led to believe.

Oh, "lead" versus "led," what confusion you two bring to the world!

Although one can "lead" today ("lead" rhyming with "freed," which could be a good reason to take action), yesterday, they would have "led" ("led" rhyming with "bed," which fits because maybe one would be tired afterward). This seems simple enough, until you realize that "lead" can also be a noun with multiple meanings and pronounced in different ways.

- "Lead" can be the position one is in, when he or she is in the front. It is another word for a dog's leash. It can be the principle actor or actress in a play, among other definitions.
- When pronounced to rhyme with "bed" or "dread," "lead" is also a type of metal, with the atomic number 82. The interior of pencils used to be made from it. Fishing sinkers, car batteries, and power line sheaths still are.

Sometimes, you have to give "lead" and "led" a second longer for consideration, and I definitely encourage you to do so. If we don't edit ourselves, crazy things can happen. Not only can your communications come out sloppy, but you could also accidentally have lead a dog with a lead lead. There are too many things wrong with that to say.

Writing Tip #89: "Let's" vs. "Lets"

When I was in 1st grade, there was a poster on the wall of bunnies in a garden, and it read "Let us eat lettuce." Why this image has stuck in my head for so many years, I cannot say. Those bunnies must have been gosh-darn cute, or maybe I was enamored with words from an incredibly young age. Either way, though, the poster gives us a lovely reminder—not only on the spelling of "lettuce," but also on the construction of the contraction "let's."

- "Let's" is a contraction, people. It's an invitation, with "let us" squished together to become "let's."
- "Lets" is a form of the verb "let," as in to allow.

Perhaps Farmer McGregor finally lets Peter Rabbit and Benjamin Bunny eat lettuce in his garden. If Farmer McGregor also had a farm-to-table restaurant, I really hope his signage would read, "Let's eat!" rather than a different option with a confused or missing apostrophe.

This mistake is commonly found at restaurants, in stores, on term papers, and beyond. It's actually a fun little scavenger hunt if you ever dare to seek it. When it comes to your own writing, however, please consider that apostrophe carefully. Don't forget it, and don't add it unnecessarily. For grammar's sake, think of those bunnies inviting you to eat lettuce. Those adorable little bunnies wouldn't want you to get this wrong.

Writing Tip #90: "Literally" vs. "Figuratively"

I know that people have been misusing the word "literally" when they mean "figuratively" in recent years, but there's a new, sad twist to the word use saga. Dictionaries have added a definition.

Traditionally:

- "Literally" has meant actually, or without exaggeration or inaccuracy.
- "Figuratively" has meant metaphorically, not literally.

You often hear people confusing the words—think Robin Scherbatsky, *How I Met Your Mother* fans ("That literally blew my mind.")—but until recently, there was always a right and a wrong.

Then came the news: many dictionaries have added a new definition to the word "literally." It may now be used for emphasis or to express strong feeling, even when something is not literally true.

What? So this second definition is the opposite of the first definition?

Perhaps, these dictionaries are okay with this. I'm not. It figuratively blows my mind. Call me a traditionalist, but I recommend avoiding this new use in your writing. Dictionaries might approve of this change, but I'm not convinced public opinion has turned that corner yet.

Writing Tip #91: "Lightening" vs. "Lightning"

Mark Twain is noted to have said, "The difference between the right word and the wrong word is the difference between lightning and the lightning bug." And he has a real point there. I'm going to take it one step further and say that it's also the difference between "lightning" and "lightening." Is my addition as clever as dear old Samuel Clemens? No. But it's an important distinction we need to make sure we understand.

"Lightening" and "lightning" are two different words, people.

- That giant bolt of static electricity once thought to be summoned by the gods is "lightning."
- The verb "to lighten" is written as "lightening" in its present participle state.

Auto-correct or spell-check won't help you with this one. You have to pay attention.

Writing Tip #92: "Like" vs. "As"

Everyone likes a good simile—especially Southerners, it seems—but whether you use "like" or "as" in your comparison is not simply a matter of taste.

To be brief:

- Use "like" when no verb follows.
- Use "as" when the following clause contains a verb.

I could get more technical and discuss prepositions and objects of the preposition versus the use of conjunctions, but that's all of the dry grammar that scares people away from English classes. I like to keep things simple.

What does this look like in action?

Example 1: That boy runs like molasses. (No verb follows, so "like" is correct.)

Example 2: That girl races as if the devil is chasing her. (A verb follows, so "as" is correct.)

If you flip-flopped these sentences, they wouldn't be correct:

Example 3: That boy runs like the devil is chasing him. (A verb follows, so "like" is incorrect.)

Example 4: That girl races as molasses. (No verb follows, so this is incorrect. Clearly.)

Okay, maybe the tricky part is when we should use "like" and when we should not. "As" isn't the problem. We like "like." We might like it too much. We might like it more than a picnic under magnolia trees complete with shoofly pie. But we have to restrain ourselves, okay?

These are the technicalities that we aren't always taught, but we have to pay attention to. Writing well requires continuing education, does it not?

Writing Tip #93: "Loath" vs. "Loathe"

I am loath to write about the words "loathe" and "loath" because no matter what I say, all some people are going to hear is hatred. And there's enough hate in the world, isn't there?

No, this pair has more to offer, albeit in its own tentative fashion. Note, these are two different words. That final "e" makes all the difference.

Remember:

- "Loathe" (with the final "e") is a verb meaning to hate. It goes beyond annoyance and dislike. If you loathe something, there is a deeper emotion brewing.
- "Loath" (without the final "e") is an adjective meaning to be reluctant or wary.

You might be loath to go to that costume party, but if you loathe costume parties, I'm wondering if there's a deeper childhood trauma lingering.

Some people are loath with the word "loath," because they aren't sure if it exists. I'm here to assure you that yes, it does; it is free of hatred. Though it might be a bit cautious at its core, all "loath" really wants is for people to realize it exists.

Writing Tip #94: "Lose" vs. "Loose"

Sure, we can be loose with our grammar sometimes, but we shouldn't lose it altogether. This is admittedly tricky when logical pronunciations don't follow certain spelling rules, but we have to take a moment, ponder what we mean to say, and get it right.

For example, "loose" is the opposite of tight. We hear that "oo" sound like in "caboose," so this is a logical spelling.

The problem comes with "lose," which, of course, is the opposite of win. It's not a rhyme for "hose" or "rose." It also has the "oo" sound, but without the double "o."

"Lose" vs. "Loose" comes down to remembering the difference. Take a moment when you're writing these two. Loose interpretations of spelling tend to lose their meaning.

Writing Tip #95: "Make Do" vs. "Make Due"

I think there might be a librarian at my local library who has magical calendar powers. She seems to make my books due sooner than I thought they were. However, outside of this wizardry, "make due" never makes sense. Got it?

The correct expression is to "make do."

I know; I hear the bafflement as you're throwing up your arms. How can these two verbs sit side by side like this and make sense?

Well, they simply do.

To "make do" means to "make [something] do well enough." (If the brackets confuse you, check out Writing Tip #156.) It means for something to be used as a perhaps lesser substitute, or sometimes it's used synonymously with "makeshift."

Although you should watch out for your own librarian with "make due" powers, do try to remember the correct form of this one, and use it accordingly.

Writing Tip #96: "Me" vs. "I"

You don't know how it feels to be "me." Wait a minute, was Tom Petty singing about grammar?

Okay, maybe not, but just for a minute, I'm going to pretend he really wrote his famous song about the misunderstood and misused word "me."

When do you use "I"? When do you use "me"? Across the world, teachers (and editors) squirm with this one every day. We really don't know how it feels to be that little word that's so often messed up. It's so short and innocent sounding. Let's make an effort to get it right once and for all, folks.

When there's more than one person in the sentence, the "I" vs. "me" decision seems to explode, so let's focus on this single piece. My favorite advice is to think about how a line would be written without the others involved.

If someone said, "Me and Tom are jamming on our guitars," (hint: not correct) I'd tell that person to remove Tom Petty from the sentence.

"Me is jamming on my guitar," he or she would respond.

Wait, what? We all hear that wording as incorrect. "I am jamming" sounds more natural for good reason. It's proper. Therefore, "Tom and I are jamming" would be correct.

This trick works for subjects and predicates alike.

"The crowd is singing along with Tom and I" might come out of some over-correcting mouths, but does "The crowd is singing along with I" really sound right? No, no, it doesn't.

"The crowd is singing along with me." Therefore, the original line should be, "The crowd is singing along with Tom and me."

Do you hear the difference? Your ear already knows. Trust it.

Ah, pronouns.

Writing Tip #97: "Might" vs. "May"

Let's look at the proper uses of "might" and "may." To narrow it down further, we're going to focus on their uses in terms of possibility.

Do you know the difference implied in the following two statements?

"We might go to the party"; "We may go to the party."

Both imply a chance, but one is a stronger chance. To help remember the difference, think of *Mighty Mouse*. When you see a superhero who is a mouse, you think there's a very slim chance of him saving the day, right? If he were an alien from the planet Krypton, maybe, but a mouse? Seriously?

This is the difference between "might" and "may."

- Use "might" when there's a possibility but a slim chance.
- Use "may" when there's a stronger likelihood.

If you "might" go to the party, no one will be holding their breath. If you "may" go, the host may add your favorite buffalo chicken dip to the spread just in case.

Of course, when we get into tense—"might have" being the past tense of "may"—we have a different discussion, but we'll leave that to another time.

Writing Tip #98: "Moral" vs. "Morale"

Morale often suffers when everyone hears they are in for a grammar lesson, but if the moral of this book is nothing else, it's that grammar doesn't have to be fall-asleep-drooling-embarrassingly-on-your-6th-grade-desk boring to be understood.

A single "e" changes the pronunciation and the meaning between these two words, and often people forget which one is which. Because simple phonetics doesn't really help, here's your reminder:

- "Moral," which rhymes with "coral" that you might see scuba diving, means either the lesson learned at the end of a story, when used as a noun, or to have a sense of integrity, when used as an adjective.
- "Morale," which rhymes with a "corral" where one might pen horses, deals with a sense of mental or emotional well-being, confidence, or enthusiasm at a given moment.

Yes, I realize my rhyming pair might need its own writing tip at a later date, but don't let it weaken your morale. There are plenty of word discoveries yet to come!

Writing Tip #99: "Myself" and Reflexive Pronouns

I've addressed the prickly "I" versus "me" usage, but "myself" needs its own moment in the editorial spotlight. Sure, it can be egotistical or dramatic, but it's time that "myself" is finally understood. Are you with me?

Above all else, remember that "myself" is not interchangeable with "I" or "me."

- The painter and myself didn't choose our palette. (Yikes!)
- No one went to the library with my friend and myself. (No!)

Neither of these sentences is correct. If you're not sure why, return to that "I" versus "me" refresher (Writing Tip #96). Here's what you do need to know about this tricky word—and let's add "yourself," "himself," "herself," "itself," "ourselves," "yourselves," and "themselves" to this conversation too. (These are all reflexive pronouns, but I'll whisper the grammar jargon so as not to scare you away.)

Reflexive pronouns have two functions:

- They either refer to a pronoun that was already used in the sentence (for example, I see myself in the mirror's reflection), or
- they add dramatic emphasis (I, myself, have caught this error more times than I can name).

That's it.

This is one we tend to overthink and overcorrect, but we need to take a step back and let "myself" and the other reflexive pronouns be themselves.

Writing Tip #100: "None Is" vs. "None Are"

Although "none" derived from the Old English word *nān*, which meant "not one," it has been used to mean either "not one" or "not any" for more than 1,000 years. During this time period, "none is" and "none are" have both been used and commonly accepted. Thus, the idea that "none" always must be followed by a singular verb is an absolute myth.

That's right; depending on the context, you may use "none is" or "none are." I hereby give you permission. No editor who is on top of his or her game will ever denounce the correct use of a plural verb after "none."

Writing Tip #101: "OK" vs. "O.K." vs. "Okay"

Sometimes, when it comes to more casual words like this, there are correct answers, and then there are correct answers for you. I'll tell you the rules; I'll tell you my preference; I'll let you decide your usage on your own. Okey dokey?

Most style guides are flexible on this spelling, commonly accepting either the "OK" or "okay" format. However, Associated Press (AP) Style, the guidebook for journalists, is one of the sticklers in this conversation, insisting upon "OK." I've also heard it said that the *New York Times* prefers "O.K."—I'm guessing the periods are for extra panache—but I haven't been able to verify that punctuation choice.

To me, "OK" seems unnecessarily formal. Maybe it's simply my aversion to the use of all CAPs (see more on this in Writing Tip #202). I don't want "OK" to be screamed at me. In almost all usages, as I'm sure you can see throughout this book, I prefer "okay."

Whichever form you use, "OK," "O.K.," or "okay" has a variety of meanings from an agreement to a declaration of something being "not too bad, not too good" to a casual transition word.

Because there are multiple correct spellings, you have a choose-your-own-adventure spelling situation on your hands. Whichever one you lean toward, there are only two major rules to follow:

- Be consistent with your style choice. You need to make up your mind and stick to it within any given writing project. If you're fluctuating between multiple forms, it's not okay.
- Only use "okay," "OK," or "O.K." in casual writing. Formal essays and business writing should have more elevated language (more on this in Writing Tip #206).

And okay, I cannot close this discussion without noting the debate around this expression's origin. The most likely story is that American slang from the early 1800s caught on and spread like wildfire due to the appropriation of "OK," standing for the playful, intentionally misspelled expression "oll korrekt," by Martin Van Buren's reelection campaign in 1840. President Van Buren's nickname was "Old Kinderhook," and his supporters became known as the "OK Club." Thus, in theory, "OK" became a part of everyday speech.

Other origin stories include Scottish, Greek, Choctaw, and French expressions, but most sources, including the Oxford English Dictionary, conclude that the American slang story is the most probable.

The "okay" spelling didn't appear until 1929, though this form actually replaced an earlier phonetic representation of the expression, "okeh," which had appeared since 1919.

You never knew there was so much to know about these two (or four) little letters, did you?

Writing Tip #102: "Onboard" vs. "On Board" vs. "Aboard"

No matter how long you've been aboard with your employer, there might not be a company excursion that involves stepping aboard a boat of any kind. Perhaps you enjoyed your "onboarding" experience, or perhaps you aren't on board with that recently coined business phrase.

You never thought about how these words could convey so many different ideas, did you?

At their essence, the discussion of "on board" and "aboard" is fairly simple, for in most cases they are synonyms. You can step on board a ship or you can step aboard a ship. Both are indeed correct, though many, including the U.S. Navy's Style Guide, seem to prefer "aboard" to "on board" when either could be used.

- Beyond the reference of being upon a train, ship, or other mode of transportation, an alternate definition for "aboard" includes becoming a member of a team (for example, Camila came aboard our team last month).
- For "on board," an alternate definition is to be comfortable with a situation (for example, we're all on board with this idea).
- Concerning "onboard" or "on-board," these are properly used only as adjectives or modifiers of something else.

They are an example of two words coming together to change their part of speech, by either squishing themselves together or by adding a hyphen between them (for more on this see Writing Tip #169). You might discuss "on-board computers" or "onboard medical services," and either of these forms would be correct.

Though I want to close this tip there, there's also the new business term "onboarding"—meaning to bring a new employee through the orientation and training process—that needs to be added into this conversation. I'm not sure if this one is a fad or business jargon here to stay, but so far it seems to be gaining popularity. Perhaps it's a verb I should finally get on board with myself.

Writing Tip #103: "Overdo" vs. "Overdue"

When you do something over, you don't "overdo" it; you "redo" it. When something needs to be returned, it's "due." When it's late, it's "overdue." When the barometric pressure has a weird effect, maybe there's such a thing as "overdew." Okay, I might have gone too far with that last one.

Admittedly, this is a pair that sometimes makes me stop and think. But remember:

- "Overdo" always involves the verb "do" as in "doing" something.
- "Overdue" always goes back to that "due date."

Am I overdoing it with these grammar tips? I hope not. Do I have any library books that are overdue? Possibly. Did my feet get wet because of some "overdew" on the grass this morning? I'm going to call artistic license on that one.

—————

Writing Tip #104: "Passed" vs. "Past"

Yes, "past" and "passed" are near-homonyms, two words that largely sound the same, but that doesn't mean they are synonyms, two words that mean the same thing.

Remember:

- "Passed" is the past tense (tricky, eh?) of "pass." It is always a verb.
- "Past" can refer to time when used as a noun or as an adjective, or it can mean beyond when used as an adverb or preposition.

Example 1: He passed by the entrance of the reptile house. ("Passed" is a verb here.)

Example 2: In the past, he'd had nightmares about snakes. ("Past" is a noun here, referring to time.)

Example 3: He passed up the opportunity to see the boa constrictor. ("Passed" is a verb here, as part of the idiom "to pass up.")

Example 4: This past year, there's been a garter snake that keeps returning to his yard. ("Past" is an adjective here, referring to time.)

Example 5: The first time he spotted it, the serpent was just past his favorite rose bush. ("Past" is a preposition here, referring to placement.)

Example 6: He had passed past the snake before he even saw what it was. ("Passed" is a verb here, and "past" is an adverb. Whoa.)

If this seems overly complicated, take a deep breath. Think about whether you want a verb or not. Is something "passing" or being "passed up"? You might want to do one last pass over this wording when you use it if you're unsure, at least until this confusion becomes something of your past.

Writing Tip #105: "Peaceable" vs. "Peaceful"

"Peaceable" is all about attitude—no, not that kind of attitude. I'm not talking about sass; I'm talking about being uninclined toward disagreement or the creation of strife. It's a state of mind, most commonly attached to people.

"Peaceful" is often linked to places and moments. If there is a sense of calm and serenity, something can be described as "peaceful."

These two words are commonly discussed as synonyms, and they nearly are—but not quite. "Peaceful" is often used to describe both people and places, but if you want to be at the top of your game, reconsider your usage. "Peaceable" is sometimes a more accurate word choice.

Writing Tip #106: "Peak" vs. "Pique" vs. "Peek"

This might peak your interest. Or is it "pique" your interest? People often feel really confident about this word—that is, until they realize they've always been wrong.

If your interest is rising, "peak" makes sense, doesn't it? Maybe. But it's not the correct usage in this case.

A "peak" is a high of some sort, real or metaphorical; however, "to pique" is the correct usage for this specific phrasing. It's from the French word *piquer* meaning "to prick" or in this case "to excite." If your curiosity is piqued, you're interested. If your curiosity is peaked, I wonder if it's really all downhill from there.

And I can't wrap up this tip without a little shout-out to the final alternate spelling of "peek," as in a quick or secretive glance. "Peeking your interest" definitely doesn't make sense. Please don't write it.

Writing Tip #107: "Pedal" vs. "Peddle" vs. "Petal"

If you sell bikes, maybe you could be a peddler of pedals. If you sell bikes with steamers and a flower-filled basket, maybe you're a peddler of pedals with petals. But whether you're in bicycle retail or not, you need to know the difference between "pedal," "peddle," and "petal."

As a reminder:

- A "pedal" is a lever or a small flat bar operated by the foot, most commonly seen in bicycles, cars, and musical instruments such as pianos.
- To "peddle" means either to sell something, often used in reference to those who travel from place to place, or to attempt to persuade others to believe something.
- A "petal" is the soft, blooming, often colorful part of the flower.

Any usage referring to feet has the same "ped-" root as "pedicure" or "biped."

Any usage referring to selling something calls back to the word "peddler." There are two "d"s there. Maybe one of them is for sale.

Any usage referring to flowers has a "t," which does slightly resemble a flower's stem.

Homonyms can indeed be tricky, but this is one I am convinced you can sort out.

Writing Tip #108: "Personal" vs. "Personnel"

It's not personal. It's business. And if it's business, maybe you need "personnel." Does that sound about right?

Have you ever had a pair of words that you really have to think hard about to remember? That's exactly what these two are for many in the business world.

Remember:

- "Personal" is most commonly an adjective meaning private or pertaining to a particular person.
- "Personnel" is a noun meaning the group of people employed in an organization.

When you're talking about "personnel," you're talking about more than one staff member, so remember that two "n"s should be there. If you're talking about something "personal," it's something unique to only one person, so there should be only one "n."

I hope that helps. Nothing personal, but it's time we straightened this one out.

Writing Tip #109: "Perspective" vs. "Prospective"

It's time to gain a little perspective on "perspective" versus "prospective." It's a business faux pas that comes up far more than it should. No matter what autocorrect thinks you're trying to say, make sure you're getting it right.

- "Perspective" has multiple meanings from how someone sees a physical view to how someone understands an idea or a situation to the depiction of spatial relationships on a flat surface.
- "Prospective," on the other hand, refers to something in the future or something that could potentially be in the future.

A human resources department might have a meeting to discuss everyone's perspective about a prospective employee. Prospective clients are often referred to as "prospects," but sales teams need to understand the prospects' individual perspectives before pursuing them if they expect to find success.

From my perspective, these two shouldn't be as confused as they often are.

Writing Tip #110: "Precede" vs. "Proceed"

Let's talk prefixes. Oh, I know it's not the sexiest of subjects, but understanding two simple prefixes will ensure you never get "precede" and "proceed" mixed up again. If you want, we can call them something besides "prefixes." We'll call them "letters fastened to the front of a word." Not much sexier and a bit more wordy, but perhaps less likely to put you to sleep.

The two sets of letters fastened to the front of a word that I want to discuss here are "pre" and "pro." I'll give you some hints, and I bet you'll be able to figure them out on your own.

- "Pre-" is used in words like "preseason," "preparty," and "preemptive." Do you notice how all of these things happen before something? Before the season, before the party, before the emptive . . . wait, no. Strike that last one. "Preemptive" means taking action in some way before something else happens, of course.
- "Pro-" is used in words like "propose," "proffer," and "provision." These are all words that look ahead, proposing something for the future, proffering something for acceptance in the future, and adding a provision to secure a future agreement.

It should be noted "pro-" can also be used as a prefix meaning to be in support of something, but that definition doesn't apply here.

With all this less than sexy but essential language knowledge in your heads, "precede" and "proceed" are now obvious, aren't they?

- "Precede" means for something to come before.
- "Proceed" means to move ahead, to go forward, or to continue.

A little linguistic dissection makes everything so much better, doesn't it? No? Anyone? Bueller?

Writing Tip #111: "Principal" vs. "Principle"

I always hated that old line, "a principal is your pal," for remembering the difference between "principal" and "principle." Sure, I really liked my elementary school principal, though I would have been nervous beyond belief if I ever was sent to her office, but even in my early years, this line seemed like a gimmick.

Vocabulary words shouldn't be advertisements for authority figures. Sure, "martinet" sounds a bit like "martini," but I think the former would be significantly less fun.

So, you can say that "a principal is your pal," but I've got a new one for you: "le prince is always principled." Of course, I'm speaking of *Le Petit Prince*. And his travels. Maybe even his time spent with a fallen pilot in the desert and their discussions of drawn sheep, rams, and boa constrictors swallowing elephants.

Is mine as catchy? Perhaps not. But it recalls a childlike innocence and integrity that we all should call to mind more often, shouldn't we?

In the end, remember:

- A "principal" is the chief or head of something or the first in rank.

- A "principle" is a moral belief that helps someone determine right or wrong, and it can also be an idea that forms
the foundation for something.

However you want to memorize these words is fine, but know that
you have options. Principals can be pals or not; le petit prince is always
principled.

––––––––––

Writing Tip #112: "Queue" vs. "Cue"

You know what's cool about the word "queue"? You can remove its last
four letters, and it's still pronounced the same way. Of course, it's also
pronounced the same way as the word "cue." Are you spelling the word
you intend to? (I'm looking at you, American writers.)
Remember:

- "Cue" (noun) means either a signal prompting an action
(for example, she entered the stage after her cue) or the
long stick used in the game of billiards.
- "Cue" (verb) means to act as a prompt or reminder (my
writing tip cued you to write "cue" correctly) or to ready a
piece of audio/video for play (he cued up the movie).
- "Queue" (noun) means a line of people waiting. It also has
definitions when it comes to computing, but those are a
bit too technical to define here.
- "Queue" (verb) means to get in line.
- "Que" is not an English word.

"Queue" and "cue" do get a bit confusing because both can be used
with the preposition "up." One can cue up something, and one can
queue up. Taking your time to remember is important, though.
Brits seem more comfortable with the difference between these
words. In the United States, people often use the "cue" form for everything. But let's be better than that, Americans, okay?

Writing Tip #113: "Raised" vs. "Rose"

Much like the difference between "lay" and "lie," we have another transitive-intransitive verb situation on our hands with "raised" and "rose." Darn it. I lost you with more grammar language again. Strike that! I meant a cat riding a skateboard! Puppies snowboarding! Donkeys driving speedboats! Are you back with me? Okay, let's dive in.

We're working with two different words: "raise" and "rise." Both mean to move upward, of course, but the difference is whether the subject is moving or the subject is moving an object.

- "Raise" is the transitive verb. (Stay with me!) It requires an object. For example, she raises her head; we raised a glass.
- "Rise" is the intransitive verb. (You've come this far. Hang on!) It doesn't require an object. For example, the sun rises in the morning; I rose out of my bed.

You can see from my examples that "raised" is the past tense of "raise," and "rose" is the past tense of "rise."

Of course, you have to keep a look out for "razed" as well, but that is another story. I'll leave that destruction to another day.

Writing Tip #114: "Real" vs. "Really"

It's time to get real. Casual-speak slips out into our writing all of the time, but this is one that irks me. "Real" is not an adverb. It shouldn't ever modify adjectives or verbs.

That girl isn't real nice. She's really nice.

That man isn't real handsome. He's really handsome.

That hedgehog isn't real adorable. It's really adorable. Unless you're saying that is what "real" adorable looks like—then, yes, a baby hedgehog is real adorable, rather than fake adorable.

"Really" is the adverb you're looking for in most of these situations. I know it's cool to abbreviate sometimes, but simply forgetting the last two letters isn't quite doing it for you.

In truth, "really" is one of those words that can often be cut to tighten and elevate your language (see Writing Tip #206 for more on that), but if you're using "real" or "really," make sure you're using the correct one.

———

Writing Tip #115: "Recur" vs. "Reoccur"

A reoccurring confusion appears about "recur" and "reoccur." Sometimes it's a matter of which one to use when. Sometimes it's a matter of realizing that these are in fact two different words.

- "Recurring" means that something happens regularly (on a schedule). A weekly meeting is a recurring meeting; a monthly bill is a recurring bill; my recurring writing tips are posted every Wednesday on my blog.
- "Reoccurring" means that something will happen again, but it's a bit more random or less scheduled. The springtime can have reoccurring thunderstorms; one might have reoccurring typos; your reoccurring reference to *Get a Grip on Your Grammar* will improve your writing skills.

This word choice comes up a lot in corporate communications. I say, impress your supervisors, and teach your team all about it. Shouldn't savvy language use be one more tactic to get ahead?

(See Writing Tip #42: "Continual" vs. "Continuous" for a similar conversation.)

Writing Tip #116: "Redundant" vs. "Repetitive"

"Redundant" and "repetitive" are a bit like "square" and "rectangle." A square is a rectangle, but a rectangle is not necessarily a square. When you are being repetitive in your writing, you are most likely being redundant; however, when you are being redundant, you aren't necessarily being repetitive.

Let's take this idea a bit further:

- For something to be "redundant," it means that it could be taken away or deleted and nothing would suffer. Airplanes, for example have a lot of intentional redundancies. If one engine goes, there is another also there. If your job has become redundant, you might not have it for long. If text in writing is redundant, perhaps you are overexplaining or being repetitive.
- For something to be "repetitive," it is being written, said, or done again.

When you write, you don't want to be redundant or repetitive, but remember that they are not the same thing. Am I being repetitive when I say this? Perhaps. I just want to drive this point home.

Writing Tip #117: "Regrettably" vs. "Regretfully"

Regrettably, many people don't know the difference between "regrettably" and "regretfully." If you're responding to an RSVP, for example, and you cannot make it, do you know which word you should use?

- If you are full of regret, be sure to use the word "regretfully." This word choice refers to someone's thoughts or feelings (including your own).

- If you are talking about a situation or action, it might be "regrettable." This word should be used when it's something that makes you feel sorry or bummed, but it isn't related to your own actions or decisions.

Ergo:

I regretfully couldn't adopt all the new kittens at the shelter.
Someone regrettably abandoned them.

As for that RSVP, be sure that you respond, "regretfully," you cannot make it. Maybe someone else will decide that it's a regrettable decision that you've made, but that shouldn't be a phrase on your reply.

Writing Tip #118: "Rein" vs. "Reign" vs. "Rain"

When it comes to these three words, most of us get them right when we're using them by themselves, but it's their idioms that get us in trouble. We know that:

- "Rain" is the water that falls from the sky, when it is a noun, or the action of water falling from the sky, when it is a verb.
- "Reign" is the either the act of ruling, as royalty does, when it is a verb, or a reference to the time period of a ruler's position as monarch, when it is a noun.
- "Rein" is either a leather strap one uses for guiding a horse, when it is a noun, or the act of guiding or holding back with either horses, people, or ideas, when it is a verb.

These are fairly simple, but then logic can get a bit scrambled when they appear in other ways. "Free reign" could be ruling with a focus on liberty for all, and "free rain" could be a haphazard freefall; however, neither is correct.

- "Free rein" is the correct idiom. It means to give someone the ability to make their own choices, like a horse with loosened reins.
- To "rein something in" also uses the "rein" form. That means to hold back. Again, think about that horse, now with tightened reins, being kept under control.

Phrases with "rain" usually are less confused. Maybe when you go dancing or when you cash your paycheck, you "make it rain." If it's pouring, it could be "raining cats and dogs." I've never caught a typo about "reigning" cats and dogs, though I wish I had. This, of course, isn't the expression, but it still puts a smile on my face. Who wouldn't love these guys with a crown?

Writing Tip #119: "Root" vs. "Rout" vs. "Route"

If you're going to "root, root, root for the home-team" and they are a football team, you can cheer as they run a route. You can follow their bus down Route 66 for an away game. En route, maybe you could even stop by dear old granddad's to show him pictures of the opponent's brutal rout. Maybe sports fanaticism is in your roots because your father and grandfather had the same passion for the team.

Confused? Don't be. There are a whole lot of meanings packed into these three words, "root," "route," and "rout," and it's time you conquer them once and for all.

Remember, there is a spelling difference in these words:

- "Root" can mean so many things. As a noun, it is the part of the plant that typically grows downward into the soil; it is the source or origin of something, including family ancestry; it is the base part of a tooth, hair, or nail; and it is a mathematical term as in "square root," among other definitions. As a verb, "root" can mean how a pig digs in the soil with its nose, to search in a cluttered area, to cheer on a team, or to lend moral support.

- "Route" can be tricky because it can be pronounced in two different ways. When "route" rhymes with "bout," as a noun, it can mean a path to travel or a regular round of stops for a job like newspaper delivery. As a verb, it can mean to forward something in a particular path or direction, be it routing cars or cables. When "route" rhymes with "boot," it refers to the specific name of a road, such as Route 66.
- "Rout" is most commonly a noun meaning an overwhelming defeat, or a verb meaning to force or drive out.

You can reroute wires or root around in your attic, but whatever you are up to with these three words, be careful with your spelling.

Writing Tip #120: "Shined" vs. "Shone"

Do you ever use the word "shone"? Technically, you should, though it's been falling out of favor lately for some reason. Whether this is grammar ignorance or a protest against shiny things, I don't know.

Admittedly, there's a debate about the usage of "shined" and "shone." Yes, the editors of the world get into the boxing ring over this one.

The most common rule is as follows:

- "Shined" is used when something is being shined. For example, "She shined the flashlight" or "He shined his shoes."
- "Shone" is used when something is shining. For example, "The sun shone brightly" or "The jewel shone with magic swirling in its core."

I'll be honest on this one, though. "Shone" isn't a word I generally use. Here's the American writer coming out in me again. I generally use "shined" in all instances. Are you aghast? Are you putting down this book, never trusting a word I say again? Or do you agree?

I told you people are at odds with this past tense pair. As a note, it's the American editors who are often the most likely to accept the use of "shined" in all instances. If you're writing for an overseas audience, you might to need to be stricter in your use.

––––––––––––

Writing Tip #121: "By" vs. "Buy" vs. "Bye"

Let's go beyond the double-negative in NSYNC's lyrics about "it ain't no lie," and talk about "bye," "by" and "buy."

Remember:

- "Bye," short for "good-bye," is a word used when separating from someone. For example, NSYNC said "bye" multiple times for emphasis to prove that they really were walking away from someone. A "bye" is also a situation where a single competitor or a team is able to move forward while skipping a game that others have to play. For example, the quarterback on my fantasy football team had a bye, so I scrambled to find a replacement.
- "By" is a preposition commonly referring to position, specifically connected with proximity; timing, in a way similar to "before"; and dimensions, as in a two by four plank or grid.
- To "buy" is to purchase or to believe. For example, you could buy tickets or buy into the boy-band craze.

NSYNC did perform along with Aerosmith, Mary J. Blige, Britney Spears, and Nelly at the 2001 Superbowl Halftime show in which no one had a bye, but I bet the admission for that night was pretty pricey to buy. And I'm not going to talk about Justin Timberlake's other Superbowl appearance. Personally, I wish he had a bye for that one.

Writing Tip #122: "Since" vs. "Because"

"Since" and "because" can be synonyms referring to causation, though it hasn't always been the case—long story, don't worry about it. The problem is that this is not the only meaning of "since."

- "Since" can refer to time (for example, I loved him since the day I heard he had a castle).
- "Since" can also refer to cause and effect just like "because" (I loved him since he was so great at kickball).

Because of this split personality, a sentence with "since" can sometimes be confusing.

Example: Since he sent the email, he was worried what she would say.

Do you see how this sentence could be read as a man concerned ever since the moment he sent the email as well as a man concerned because he sent the email? Oh, English language, why do you have to be so confusing?

In short, when it comes to choosing between "since" and "because," do your best to avoid ambiguity. Even when you know exactly what you're expressing, someone else might be unsure. (For more on writing with clarity, see Writing Tip #190.)

Make sure that your words are crystal clear before using "since" referring to causation. If you're sure it's clear, go for it. If not, know that "because" is always a suitable option.

Writing Tip #123: "Sneaked" vs. "Snuck"

If you were to be sneaky and take a cookie from the cookie jar, would you say that you "sneaked" or "snuck"? There was one right answer a few centuries ago. Today, the answer is a little bit more flexible.

Although some old-fashioned grammarians might argue that one must always use "snuck" as the proper past tense of "sneak," this argument is becoming rarer by the day. It still has its stronghold in Great Britain, but from its first use in the 1800s, "sneaked" has sneaked into our everyday vernacular.

You can absolutely get away with this newer word form. Don't let someone tell you that "snuck" is the only past tense that is acceptable.

Writing Tip #124: "Sometime" vs. "Some Time" vs. "Sometimes"

Sometimes, when I have some time, I wonder if I should take up rock climbing again sometime. Did you catch the three different usages in that line—not to mention my adventurous side?

- "Sometime" is an adverb that means at some indeterminate point in time in the future (for example, do you want to join me sometime?).
- "Sometimes" is an adverb meaning now and then (sometimes, I get itchy to get outside if I sit at my desk for too long).
- "Some time" is simply the two words, "some" and "time," next to each other (if I take some time to make a plan, I could probably build a fun adventure).

Sometimes we have typos with these words because we touch the wrong key on the keyboard, and sometimes these typos come because we forget the difference. Give it some time. If you do, you're sure to get them right.

Writing Tip #125: "Spilt" vs. "Spilled"

Why could you argue that the word choice is correct when one "spilled the beans" about the "crying over spilt milk"? Well, in essence, it's all a matter of the dates and locations of the two idioms' origins. Let's dive into "spilt" versus "spilled."

Although "spilt" was the original past tense form of the verb "spill," the most commonly used past tense form today is "spilled." It's this newer form I recommend to you for no reason other than it's the one that has fallen into style.

As we know from discussions of "shined" and "shone" (see Writing Tip #120), verb forms sometimes evolve. The "spilt" and "spilled" shift seems to have happened in American English first—in the early 1900s—and then afterward in British English, though the latter still gives occasional love to "spilt."

Getting back to my original question, the expression "spilled the beans" was first noted in an American newspaper, the *Stevens Point Journal*, in a 1908 article discussing sneaky politicians. (Oh how times haven't changed . . .)

"Crying over spilt milk" finds its first written usage in 1659 in James Howell's British publication *Paroimiografia*.

Thus, if you were to stay true to the era of these idiom's origins, you would speak of "spilled beans" and "spilt milk."

Yes, "spilled" is the better form to use in most instances these days, but you have to admit, a little burst of language nostalgia is sometimes fun. And this idiom about milk is one of the few places you can still write "spilt" without raising too many American eyebrows.

Writing Tip #126: "Suppose to" vs. "Supposed to"

No matter how frequently I see it, I cannot accept "suppose to" in lieu of "supposed to." I understand that when we speak quickly, we sometimes don't pronounce that "d," but when we write, we need to be more precise.

Please always write "supposed to," and never "suppose to."

Your writing is supposed to show off your best, so make sure you get these details right.

Writing Tip #127: "Taut" vs. "Taught"

At the end of the school year, some teachers might feel like their nerves are taut after the long hours of dedication to all of the students they've taught. They might feel even more stressed if they caught this typo. Sure, the mathematicians might not blink and the history teachers might just shake their heads. But the English and composition teachers might begin to twitch, and really, don't they deserve better?

It's one of those mistakes that irony tied up in a pretty little bow. We should all be taught the differences between "taught" and "taut," shouldn't we?

- "Taught" is the past tense of "teach."
- "Taut" is to be stretched out or pulled tight.

If you've never officially been taught the difference between "taught" and "taut," let that end here. I want to say you've been schooled, but that just doesn't seem right either.

Writing Tip #128: "Teenage" vs. "Teen-age" vs. "Teenaged"

Uh oh, did the *Teenage Mutant Ninja Turtles* get it wrong? Some stuffy grammarians might raise their noses, insisting these were "teenaged" mutant ninja turtles. In fact, that was the first form of the word and therefore correct, they'd say. But don't listen. They're wrong.

I don't know what it is about this word in particular, but for some reason many people insist that "teenaged" came first. My guess is that they're making a connection to words like "ice(d) tea," "skim(med) milk," or "whip(ped) cream," where the final "d" has been lost with time. However, the first use of "teen-age" was in 1921. "Teen-ager" first arrived in 1941, and "teen-aged" didn't appear until 1952. Of course, the hyphen was lost through time too (as often happens, see Writing Tip #215 for more on this idea).

So what does this all mean when it comes to what form is correct? In American English, "teenage" is the most common and most accepted form. Don't call out those ninja turtles—not that you'd want to anyway. They'd probably win the fight.

Writing Tip #129: "Than" vs. "Then"

Do you often confuse "than" with "then"? Remember:

- "Than" is used in a comparison;
- "Then" is used to show passage of time.

Example: He knew his grammar was better than his friends'. He often saw flawed social media posts then added names to his running list of offenders.

Whether this is building up to a grammarian horror flick or a mental breakdown amid bleeding red pens, I don't know. Feel free to finish the story however you see fit.

———

Writing Tip #130: "That" vs. "Which"

Yes, there really is a time you should use "that" and a time you should use "which," though most people aren't aware of it.

The difference between using an adjective clause that starts with "that" and one that starts with "which" depends on whether it is a restrictive clause or not. I'm sure I don't need to go any further because grammar jargon is so user-friendly and self-explanatory . . . but just in case I do, think of a restrictive clause as one that is essential to the meaning of the sentence. For example, "Frogs that sing and dance are talented." If you take out "that sing and dance," you still have a complete sentence, but a sentence that lost its original meaning. The writer in this instance is talking specifically about "frogs that sing and dance" as being talented, not all frogs.

Nonrestrictive clauses do not contribute to the greater meaning of the sentence. For example, "Frogs, which are amphibians, start their lives as tadpoles." Do you see how the "which are amphibians" clause could be removed and nothing would be lost? It adds information, but isn't essential to the total sentence.

So in conclusion, with a clause that has to be there for the sentence to make sense, use "that." With a clause that could be removed with no meaning lost from the sentence, use "which." This explains why "which" clauses should be surrounded by commas and "that" clauses should not. Make sense?

Furthermore, did you know that Warner Brothers' singing and dancing frog is named "Michigan J. Frog"? I did not. There you go.

Writing Tip #131: "That" vs. "Who"

When you're writing a story about anthropomorphic animals, you have an option of whether you want to refer to the creatures as if they were people or not. When you're telling a story about your pet, you have a similar grammatical choice to make. Do you refer to them as if they were human, or do you refer to them like they are not?

I know when it comes to Alexander the Grrrrreat, it's a question that can pull on your heart strings. Why wouldn't he ever be considered anything other than a full member of the family, pronoun choice included? Let's dive in and see.

As any writer knows, if you would like to give more information about a person, place, thing, or idea, and you need more than an adjective or two to do so, an adjective clause that starts with "who," "that," or "which," gives you more room to play.

Refer to Writing Tip #130 for further discussion of "that" vs. "which" and essential phrases, but let's focus on "who" versus "that" for a moment.

- Use "who" only when referring to a person or a group of people (for example, the man who sold you the puppy or the people who breed Finnish Spitz dogs). Note, you can learn more about "Who" vs. "Whom" in Writing Tip #149.
- "That" is a bit more flexible according to some, but the easiest rule of thumb to follow is that "that" is used in cases not referring to people (for example, the chew toy that the puppy loves or the food that used to be in the bowl).

Are these the subtle English-language writing rules designed just to see who is paying attention? Perhaps. But since you are, please follow suit.

As for Alexander the Grrrrreat, there are exceptions to every rule, and maybe he's one.

Writing Tip #132: "Thaw" vs. "Unthaw"

When it comes to thawing, there's potential for your hands to get dirty. Sometimes, the hazard is E. coli on your kitchen counter. Sometimes, it's a matter of messy letters that dirty your writing.

Have you ever wondered why "thaw" and "unthaw" mean the exact same thing? You pull out tomorrow's chicken to thaw, or you pull it out to let it unthaw. This pairing isn't logical, yet these two words are used to mean the same thing commonly across North America.

My recommendation: stick to "thaw." There might still be concerns for contamination, but at least no letters will go to waste.

Writing Tip #133: "Themselves" vs. "Theirselves"

"Theirselves" is not actually a word. It sometimes sneaks into everyday vernacular, just like "hisself" does on occasion, but please strike these words from your vocabulary. Made-up words, no matter how common, do little to help you communicate as well as you could.

Writing Tip #134: "There" vs. "They're" vs. "Their"

There, there, dear reader, don't be distraught by the spelling of "there," "their," and "they're" anymore. This has to be the most confused set of words in the English language. Social media would practically shut down if posts with this typo were denied. Am I exaggerating? Maybe. But just a little bit.

Here's a quick review:

- "There" is a place (for example, I want to go there). Hint: you'll find the word "here" inside of "there." Both of these words are places. If you can swap out "here" for "there" in your sentence, you need this t-h-e-r-e form.
- "They're" is a contraction meaning "they are." Why do contractions continue to baffle us? The world will never know.
- "Their" is a possessive pronoun (for instance, That was their dog). Hint: you'll find the word "heir" inside of "their." And an heir has lots of stuff to possess, right?

You'll remember now, won't you? Please? Don't make me appeal to the social media powers that be. I hear grammarians have some pull. Maybe. I tell myself (sigh).

As an added bonus (I know you're excited! Grammar extras! Woot woot!), let's toss "there's" and "theirs" into the mix. Remember, these words follow the same there/they're/their rules as above.

- "There's" is a contraction, short for "there is" (There's rain on the horizon. Where? There. Not here.).
- "Theirs" is another form of the third-person possessive case (Theirs are the perfectly crafted social media posts.).

I have faith you can get these words right. Don't let me down!

Writing Tip #135: "Threw" vs. "Through" vs. "Thru"

It has come to my attention that "thru" has slipped into the business world. Repeatedly. I know I'm not the only one cringing.

Remember:

- "Through" is a preposition.
- "Threw" is a verb, the past tense of "throw."

Yes, "thru" seems ubiquitous from fast food chains to major news network Twitter feeds (twitch, wince . . . deep breath), but this is an abbreviation that simply is not appropriate for the workplace.

To help you remember these differences, let's think about a fast food chain employee exasperated by customers' bad grammar. One day, he was so annoyed, he threw (verb) food through (preposition) the drive-thru (annoying abbreviation) window. See the variance? And don't you love that a word like "defenestration" exists?

Writing Tip #135.1

"Defenestration" (noun) is the act of throwing something through a window.

Writing Tip #136: "To" vs. "Two" vs. "Too"

When we type quickly, our fingers sometimes get spelling amnesia. That's my theory, and I'm sticking ~~two too~~ to it.

Take the time to edit yourself, and remember the spellings you learned a long, long time ago:

- "To" is most commonly a preposition (for example, from here to there; east to west; pedal to the metal).
- "Two" is a noun or an adjective, what one plus one equals.
- "Too" is an adverb, meaning "also" or "extremely."

Are there more subtleties to these words? Sure. But we're not getting into those at the moment. Remember the basics, and please don't only rely on spell-check. Spell-check isn't always your friend.

Writing Tip #137: "Toward" vs. "Towards"

I'm not one who can don a believable British accent, so maybe that's why I always use "toward" and not "towards." You don't know what I'm talking about? This is another case of regional differences.

The choice of "toward" or "towards" is not a matter of right or wrong. Usually, it's a matter of geography. Across the pond, "towards" is more common—as are related forms: "backwards," "forwards," "upwards," "afterwards," etc.

In the United States, "toward" is more common—as are "backward," "forward," "upward," "afterward," etc.

I guess I'm conventional and follow the crowd on this one—my crowd being American. Either one you choose, though, make sure you're consistent about it. If your writing waffles between the two, it's jarring not only for your reader, but also for your national identity. There's no such thing as a grammatical dual-citizen.

Writing Tip #138: "Travesty" vs. "Tragedy"

You could argue that it's a travesty of the English language when we confuse "travesty" and "tragedy." These words shouldn't be used interchangeably.

- A "tragedy" is a calamity or disaster, something lamentable. It has its roots in theatre as a description of a play without a happy ending, where the main character often suffers his or her downfall. The original Greek word was *tragōidía*, which came from *trágos* (goat) + *ōide* (song). Whether this goat's song refers to the god Bacchus, costumed actors in goat-skins, the prize of a goat for the best show, or the tragedy of a goat's singing voice is up for debate.

- A "travesty" is a grotesque imitation or mockery of something, a burlesque of something serious. It shares its Latin origin with the word "transvestite," specifically *trā*, which is a variant of *trāns* (across) + *vestīre* (to cloth). The present English usage seems to have come out of the French *travestir,* to disguise, in roughly 1674.

Romeo and Juliet is a tragedy. A tornado's destruction is a tragedy. On the other hand, you might hear of a "travesty of justice" in a court trial where the rules seem to have been bent, thus creating a mockery of the justice system. A rigged election is a travesty. An unfortunate lip synch can be too.

Travesties can be tragedies, but it isn't always so. Being careful with this usage can avoid results that fall into either category.

Writing Tip #139: "Try and" vs. "Try to"

Some people like to cause a big stink around certain expressions, insisting that there is a right answer; however, when it comes to "try and" and "try to," there is no wrong answer necessarily.

There's a subtle distinction between "try and" and "try to" if you think about it. If you try and write a book, it's a bit different from trying to write a book. The former implies a degree of success. You tried, and you wrote it. Two distinct verbs are being used. The latter phrase, "try to write a book," is simply showing the effort. What are you trying to do? You're trying to write a book. There's no degree of success implied.

Some argue that "try to" is a more formal construction than "try and," or that "try and" is simply a wordy phrasing. As for me, I think they both have their place as long as the writer understands the difference.

Then there's always Yoda who would probably want to discount either phrase. He did say, "Do or do not. There is no try," in *The Empire Strikes Back* after all.

Writing Tip #140: "Unique" and Other Absolute Modifiers

Something is either unique or it isn't. Degrees of uniqueness are illogical.

Example 1: It was the most unique snowflake of Christmas morning. (Incorrect. What makes it more unique than other unique snowflakes?)

Example 2: A unique snowflake fell upon the fur of a bouncing bumblebee. (Correct.)

Unique is an example of an absolute modifier (stay with me!) or a word that doesn't have degrees. Other examples include the words perfect, rare, identical, straight, fatal, immortal, opposite, and complete.

Something cannot be "very perfect" or "more perfect." Perfect is simply perfect. Some identical twins are not more identical than others. Identical means identical. A road cannot be more straight than another straight road; an injury cannot be more or less fatal; a god cannot be degrees more immortal than another; a complete opposite is no different than any other opposite. You see what I mean, right?

Some adjectives require no further explanation, so please stop muddling them with extra descriptors. It doesn't make you more unique or your writing more complete.

Writing Tip #141: "Until" vs. "Till" vs. "'Til"

Quick, think fast. Which of these three is the oldest form of the word? Have your answer? Are you sure?

I'll be honest. I assumed the wrong answer for a long time, and this assumption led me to dark, ungrammatical places. Not so scary, perhaps, but not a place any writer wants to be.

Okay, ready?

The first known use of "till" in its present meaning of "up to the time when" was before the year 800 in Old English. That's right: "till" is the oldest of the three words. "Until" didn't arrive until the twelfth century, combining the known "till" with the prefix of "un" (or more specifically the Norse "und") in the same manner that brought us "unto" (a bit outdated, but Shakespeare would approve).

In the present day, of course, "until" is considered the standard. Using "till" or "'til" is considered more casual. Somewhere, we've gotten it into our heads that 'til is the proper abbreviated form of "until," but this is a newer, not universally accepted form. It seems logical, sure, but the double-Ls win the day.

In your writing, I recommend "until" in most situations, but know that when you want to use a shorter form, "till" is the way to go. This is one of those respecting our elders moments, I think.

Now who had that answer right?

Writing Tip #142: "Use to" vs. "Used to"

Psst . . . I think you've forgotten a letter. Again.

- Remember, "used to" is a phrasing you use to discuss something that has already happened. Ergo, it is always in past tense: "used to."
- In other instances, "use" and "to" can be friendly neighbors explaining that you can utilize something for the purpose of something else (see my earlier sentence).

This is all simple enough, you say. Thanks for the reminder, you say, but then comes the tricky part you might not have seen coming.

The form of "used to" changes if you're posing a question. Didn't you use to like magicians? Just like that, the required "d" disappears.

"Used to" also should lose the "d" when you're using it in the negative. You didn't use to think this was so complicated, did you?

And it's not complicated really. There are simply a few specifics that you need to be aware of, specifics that probably roll off of your tongue naturally when you speak, but sometimes make your fingers stutter on the keyboard when you are typing.

However, that's something that used to happen to you. Not anymore, right?

Writing Tip #143: "Verses" vs. "Versus"

For bailiffs, bards, or others who have stumbled, here's a quick refresher.

- "Verses" is a plural noun, referring to writing with meter and rhythm, as in a song or a poem.
- "Versus" is a preposition used to highlight a confrontation or opposition.

As much fun as it is to see reference to a poet's "versus" (was Marlowe really Shakespeare's arch nemesis?) or a court case in song ("Brown verses the Board of Education" might be a sweet ballad, no?), people should probably edit themselves more closely.

Writing Tip #144: "Vulnerable" vs. "Venerable"

These two words are so close and yet so far away. I could understand a great old sage who lives atop a mountain being described as "venerable." If he's "vulnerable," maybe he needs some bodyguards, some safety railings, or some major doses of vitamin C.

- To be "vulnerable" means susceptible of being hurt, damaged, or to be openly in danger. This can be physical danger, moral danger, or otherwise. This mountain-top sage could be vulnerable when his visitors have hidden weapons, when he walks too close to the cliff's edge, or when he's exposed to the flu virus.
- To be "venerable" is to be highly esteemed due to wisdom, age, or position. The wise old man of the mountain would be venerable, as would the wise old woman of the mountain next door.

Both of these words come from Latin, but they do not share the same root. "Vulnerable" comes from *vulnerābilis*, which means wounding. "Venerable" comes from *venerābilis*, which means worthy of veneration or reverence.

Humorous malapropisms pop up when these two are swapped, from a vulnerable pope to a venerable runt of the litter. Yes, interesting stories could be made up for either of these examples, but I'm guessing that wasn't the original goal of either statement.

Be careful with "venerable" and "vulnerable," everyone!

Writing Tip #145: "Wait on" vs. "Wait for"

When English sometimes baffles those of us who speak it as our first language, sometimes I feel sorry for those who are learning it later in life. Sometimes, the subtleties can catch you, distort meanings, or show off your lack of expertise—no matter when you learned it.

There is a difference between "waiting on" my great-aunt Anastasia and "waiting for" my great-aunt Anastasia. Do you know what it is?

Hint: if you've ever worked at a restaurant, you probably waited on a lot of customers. Hopefully, you didn't have to wait for your paycheck too long.

- When one "waits on" something or someone, this means that he or she is in a serving or subservient role. A waiter waits on the people at the tables. A prisoner might wait on a dragon queen.
- When one "waits for" something or someone, this refers to the process of being inactive until something happens, someone shows up, or similar. You can wait for your bus, or you can wait for your birthday. If your Great Aunt Anastasia still hasn't arrived, maybe you're waiting for her.

Should I wait up to see if you have any questions on this one?

Writing Tip #146: "Wary" vs. "Weary"

I know a lot of people get so nervous around this pairing that they choose to use different words altogether, but not you, grammar-savvy readers.

You know that:

- "Wary" means to be cautious.
- "Weary" means to be tired.

To nicely confuse things, "leery" rhymes with "weary" but is actually a close synonym of "wary."

Ah, the English language.

Writing Tip #147: "Whether" vs. "Weather" vs. "Wether"

It has recently been brought to my attention that "wether" is not necessarily an incorrect spelling, because a "wether" is a castrated goat or sheep. Did I know this? No, I did not. My guess is, though, that this isn't quite the word most writers intend to use . . . unless there's this massive farm animal story genre that I'm not aware of.

The real decision probably comes down to the use of "weather" or "whether." I'm fairly certain that most know the difference between these two words and that it's fast typing and auto-correct bringing people down. If I'm wrong, don't tell me. Let me keep my faith.

Remember:

- "Weather" refers to the conditions outside.
- "Whether" is a word used when considering two or more alternatives.

"Wether" really isn't the word you want to use. I'm 99 percent confident on that.

―――――――――

Writing Tip #148: "While" vs. "As"

No offense to William Faulkner, but I think he got one of his most famous titles wrong—then again, *While I Lay Dying* doesn't really have the same ring to it. The difference between "while" and "as" seems to be little-known, but there is a difference.

As you know, both words denote simultaneous action, but do you know the difference in the following two sentences?

Example 1: As Erin petted her cat, she wondered about word choice.

Example 2: While Erin petted her cat, she wondered about word choice.

At first glance, they seem to say the same thing; however, one of these is a brief action, and one is longer. Erin either patted her cat on the head and walked away, or she cuddled up on her couch with her cat for the evening, continually stroking its fur while reading a good book. Word usage tells us the difference.

To be specific:

- "As" is used for a short action.
- "While" is used for a longer one.

Example 3: As Faulkner picked up his pen, he debated his title.

Example 4: While Faulkner wrote his book, he debated a grammatical rebellion.

It doesn't take long to pick up a pen. It does, however, take a long time to write a book. See the difference?

In *As I Lay Dying*, Addie's death is a slow one, not immediate; therefore, "while" should be the appropriate word choice. But we can chalk this up to artistic license. We can give Faulkner that.

As a closing note, I like to believe that the usage of "Lay" in this title is simply the past tense of "Lie." If it's present tense, we have another lay/lie debate on our hands (see Writing Tips #86 and #87 for more on this). Oh, the dramas of word choice!

Writing Tip #149: "Who" vs. "Whom"

Lots of people treat the word "whom" like that crazy wife in the attic, knowing her secrets but not uttering her name. Are you one of them? Or have the differences between "who" and "whom" never really been explained to you?

"Who" and "whom" are both considered pronouns. Understanding their usages is easiest if you understand the difference between subjects and objects in a sentence. If your eyes started to glaze over, I'll make it even simpler.

Think about where you would use "he" versus "him" in answering a question. "Whom" ends in "m"; "him" ends in "m." Use it as a reminder.

Q: Who was at the door? A: He was at the door.

Q: Whom did you go with? A: I went with him.

Q: Who let the dogs out? A: He let the dogs out.

Q: Whom do you believe? A: I believe him.

It's not really as complicated as many seem to think. Don't be a victim of grammatical snobbery (or evasion). Command your "who" and "whom" with pride.

Writing Tip #150: "Who's" vs. "Whose"

Who's on first? Whose shoes are those? Who's that girl? Whose slice of cheesecake is that? Can I have it?

Wait, before I get distracted by my sweet tooth, let's dive into the differences between "who's" and "whose." Logic doesn't always apply easily to grammar. This one—like "its" and "it's" (see Writing Tip #84)—is another exception to the rule that possessives have the apostrophe "s."

- "Who's" is a contraction—just like can't, you're, or y'all—short for "who is" or sometimes "who was" or "who has."
- "Whose" is the possessive form.

Yes, it's true. Every time you've assumed "who's" was possessive, you've been wrong. Hopefully, those were emails to your friends, not your boss's boss's boss. My fingers are crossed for you.

Writing Tip #151: "Yeah" vs. "Yay" vs. "Yea"

"Yeah, it's time to decorate for Christmas."

How do you read this sentence? Is it full of enthusiasm or badly hidden chagrin? This isn't a judgment of your holiday spirit. It's a judgment of your spelling.

To answer the question: Scrooge McDuck was never so casual with his speech, but the above line is more fitting for him than for your child's Elf on a Shelf. (Yes, I said "McDuck." Sorry, Charles Dickens, but the old Disney version will always be my favorite.)

Remember:

- "Yeah" is a casual "yes."
- "Yay" is vocalized jubilation.
- "Yea" is the opposite of "nay" (for *Robert's Rules of Order* fans).

Got it? Good. And good luck with those decorations this year.

Writing Tip #152: "Yolk" vs. "Yoke"

Don't have egg on your face after you've realized you've mistyped "yolk" and "yoke." There's an entirely different discussion I want to have about the origin of this phrase. Does it come from the unfortunate actors of the 1800s who were pelted with eggs because they had such poor performances? Does it come from thieving barnyard animals who give themselves away by the mess that still lingers on their snouts? Does it come from sloppy eaters of breakfast? I really want to know, but I can't seem to figure it out.

Idiom etymology aside, remember:

- A "yolk" is the yellow center of an egg. There's a lot of science I won't go into here concerning embryos and their nourishment.
- A "yoke" is a frame that fits the neck and shoulders to harness an animal to put it to work. It can also be used metaphorically on subjects such as slavery.

There's also a really cheesy laugh that sounds similar—yuk, yuk, yuk—but I don't think that's related.

Writing Tip #153: "You're" vs. "Your"

Don't confuse "your" with "you're." I think we all know the difference, but, wow, is this one muddled a lot.

- "Your" is possessive.
- "You're" is the contraction of "you are."

Know it; love it; don't let your fast typing betray your intelligence.

Punctuation

Oh, I saw you start to close this book. Wait! Stop! This is important, I promise!

The rules of punctuation are logical and clearly defined. I could write another book on only this subject (and perhaps I will), but consider the following 17 punctuation tips a simple primer.

There was a moment in history centuries ago when writers realized that words alone could not convey an entire message. These words needed to be adorned with symbols that brought them to life, surrounded by points that made them show their true colors, and intertwined with marks that sometimes conjoined them or sometimes carved them apart.

They are just dots, lines, and squiggles, people. Nothing to be afraid of. You can indeed conquer them once and for all.

Writing Tip #154: Semicolons

No one seems to know how to use semicolons. They're the misused and abused punctuation mark, often thrown down without much thought, but they should have some dignity.

Let's talk about that semicolon kind of life.

Semicolons should only be used in three situations:

- They separate complete sentences. Always make sure that you have complete sentences on both sides of the semi-colon. You can combine two or more complete sentences in this way; there's no real limit (for example, The song "Semi-Charmed Life" by Third Eye Blind was a 90s standard; I never realized that song talked about doing meth; you're looking up the lyrics now, aren't you?).
- They separate items in a complicated list. The definition of a complicated list is any list that has commas within it (for example, Some of the biggest Third Eye Blind songs that come to mind include "Semi-Charmed Life," released in 1997; "Jumper," released in 1997; and "How's It Going To Be," also released in 1997.).
- They make great winky faces ;)

Please stop using semicolons where dashes or commas make more sense. Throwing them in haphazardly doesn't make you look smarter, I promise.

Writing Tip #155: Colons

Allow me to be your colon specialist. Wait, strike that. I don't want to put myself in that position. No, instead, allow me to be your double-dotted punctuation advisor.

Colons are useful little fellows, so useful in fact, that people tend to throw them in far more than they are actually needed.

Most people are comfortable with the everyday uses of a colon:

- To separate the chapter and verse of a Bible reference (Corinthians 13:4).
- To show a ratio (10:1 odds).
- To show a subtitle (*Get a Grip on Your Grammar: 250 Writing and Editing Reminders for the Curious or Confused*).
- To separate hours and minutes (1:17 a.m.).
- To end a formal salutation in a business letter (Dear Ms. Spisak:).

Yet when colons start being introduced into sentences, a small panic sometimes ensues.

Beyond the previous list, a colon is used properly only in the following scenarios:

- To show a list after a complete sentence.
- To direct attention to a quotation after a complete sentence.
- To show further information about a noun or noun phrase at the end of a complete sentence.
- To give further explanation about a complete sentence.

Are you noticing a trend? I'm really hoping that you are.

Let's look at some correctly placed colons in action.

Example 1: I often have trouble remembering the names of the nine muses: Calliope, Clio, Euterpe, Thalia, Melpomene, Terpsichore, Erato, Polyhymnia, and Urania. (Correct. Notice how there is a complete sentence preceding the list.)

Example 2: For the many writers who believe in the Muse, we can blame the words of the Greek poet Hesiod: "Happy is the man whom the Muses love: sweet speech flows from his mouth." (Correct. Notice how the section before the quotation could stand on its own.)

Example 3: Hesiod only left the world two completed works: these being *Works and Days* and *Theogony*. (Correct. Notice how "two completed works," which is at the end of a complete sentence, is further clarified after the colon.)

Example 4: Hesiod's translated tales are commonly read in school, but most often people remember the stories rather than his name: the Greek myths we know come largely from his work. (Correct. Notice how there is a complete sentence before the further information that relates directly to the complete sentence.)

Hint: People tend to stick colons after "such as," "for example," "including," and "are." But you know better than this, don't you?

I know sprinkling extra dots into your sentences sometimes looks festive, but try to restrain yourselves and use your colons only as intended. That's the advice of your double-dotted punctuation advisor anyhow. The Muses will appreciate it too.

Writing Tip #156: Parentheses vs. Brackets (and Braces too!)

We all know (and love) parentheses, but I wonder if you know when to use related punctuation. Brackets, for example, are handier for more than just playoffs. And what about braces? Where do they fit into the equation?

Bonus question: do you know where brackets and braces are found on your keyboard? Did you just look?

Parentheses

Parentheses are used within sentences to include nonmandatory information that adds to the sentence. So in other words, if you took that information out, nothing would be lost from the sentence.

Brackets

There are two main purposes for brackets within sentences. My scholar or journalist readers know the first one, the case of using brackets to insert changes into a quotation for the sake of clarity and/or grammatical correctness. This is different from the use of ellipses. If, for example, you had a source tell you, "It changed my life," a writer might have to clarify that sentence for an audience. The quote might then appear, "[Kris's book] changed my life." If you wrote this line, "It (Kris's book) changed my life," the parenthetical section would look as if it appeared in the original source.

This bracket insertion into a quote is also commonly seen when a writer adds in [sic]. Have you ever seen this and then thrown your hands up into the air, shouting "Et tu, dead Latin language!" No? Okay, well that's a good thing. If you've ever wondered what this addition meant, "sic" is short for *sic erat scriptum* or "thus it was written." It's a polite way to call out a mistake in a quotation and clarify that this was not a typo on the part of the more recent writer. For example, if you were quoting Dan Quayle, maybe you would say, the former vice president wrote, "I like a good potatoe [sic]."

So, in sum, bracket function #1: Use brackets to add clarity inside a quotation.

Bracket function #2: Use brackets inside of parentheses for the sake of clarity, in the same way that you use single quotations inside of double quotations. (Did I just throw you? If so, stay tuned for Writing Tip #161). If you ever have a side note within a side note, brackets can be useful. It's rare, but it's good to know in case you need it. We all know grammar emergencies come up.

Braces

For those who really like tangents, you can use braces, built for side notes within side notes within side notes (I'm not joking [though it

looks a bit crazy {crazy!}]). So, yes, braces are for more than straighten-
ing your teeth, but I wouldn't recommend them for everyday use.

Don't you feel informed now?

———

Writing Tip #157: Avoid the Blackout Comma

I'll admit it: I'm an Oxford comma groupie (if you didn't get that from
me already). But there's a methodology to my comma zealotry. There's
a difference between correctly comma-ing and looking like you're
drunk. (And yes, "comma-ing" is a word. I just made it up, but I'm
holding to it.)

In my book (that is, my opinion, not my actual book), there is
pocket dialing, drunk texting, and what I dub "the blackout comma."
Why are they there? What is the logic? It's a mystery that only the
writer once knew. And he or she may not remember now.

Comma reminders:

- Do not use commas with lists of two (for example, "he
  ran, and biked" is incorrect).
- Do not use commas between subject and predicate ("my
  brilliant and savvy grammar teacher, was awesome" is
  incorrect).
- Do not use commas around "essential people" ("Author,
  Kris Spisak, loves the intricacies of grammar" is incorrect—
  See Writing Tip #158 for more on this).
- Do not use commas between adjectives of number, size
  and/or color ("the four, big, black, and white tires" is
  incorrect).
- Do not use commas to add a dramatic pause where punc-
  tuation is otherwise illogical ("Oh, my, goodness, Becky.
  Did you see, that huge, typo" is incorrect).

Sure, we all slip and have one comma too many on occasion. It
happens to the best of us. I just feel like I've seen a lot of intoxication

lately. Consider me your punctuation sponsor. It's all about moderation, people.

———————

Writing Tip #158: Commas With "Essential" vs. "Nonessential" People

The delineation of people into essential versus nonessential categories sounds a bit like something out of a John Hughes flick, doesn't it? But I'm not talking social strata. I'm talking commas and restrictive clauses. Take that, Claire Standish.

Have you ever wondered why sometimes writers surround appositives with commas and sometimes they don't? Let me rephrase that. Have you ever started reading something, come across the word "appositives," and then debated whether you should keep reading because you a) didn't know what it meant and/or b) started feeling a grammar-induced yawn coming on?

Stay with me. This is a helpful one.

First things first, an "appositive" is a noun placed next to another noun for the sake of identification. Often, these are names (for example, Liu Wei, my neighbor; Frieda, the restaurant owner; Betty, an organic chicken farmer; etc). Whether or not these names are surrounded by commas—as they were in each of my cases—is decided by whether that name is "essential" to the sentence as a whole. In other words, if you took out the appositive, would the sentence still make sense? If so, it belongs in commas. If not, keep it out.

Example 1: Early on in *The Breakfast Club*, the princess, Claire Standish, says she wouldn't talk to any of her fellow detention-mates in school on Monday because they weren't on her social level. (Note, you could remove the appositive—"Claire Standish"—and no meaning would really be lost. A princess is a princess.)

Example 2: Director John Hughes released *The Breakfast Club* in 1985. (Note, if you took out the appositive—"John Hughes"—the sentence would be a bit confusing. In this case, the appositive is essential.)

But then again, when isn't John Hughes essential? Is it just me? I don't think so.

Writing Tip #159: Where to Put Commas With Greetings

Commas, colons, the vocative case . . . who knew a simple hello was so complicated?

It's not actually. How to punctuate a greeting is really quite easy to remember—never mind if your email inbox argues otherwise.

Remember, "dear" is not a greeting like "hello." Dear is an adjective, a modifier of the name that follows. "Dear Lauren" is no different from "My dearest Lauren," "Darling Clementine," or some similarly old fashioned but enchantingly romantic greeting that has faded out of favor. (Who wants to bring it back with me? Anyone? Anyone?)

If you're beginning a message with "Hi," "Hello," "Good morning," "Hola," or any other greeting, however, you should include a comma before the name of the message's recipient. We learned about the vocative case in middle school (maybe), which directs writers to use a comma before a person's name when they are being talked to.

Example 1: Throw me the ball, Peyton.

Example 2: Hi, Mr. Manning.

It's the same form in a greeting.

Lazy punctuation has become pretty widespread, though. In email, skipping this comma has largely become the norm. I see that argument when you don't want to be too formal, but this is still a rule worth understanding.

Hint: As noted in Writing Tip #155, a colon can also be used in place of a comma at the end of a salutation in formal letters.

Writing Tip #160: Where to Skip Commas in Adjective Lists

Let's talk about punctuation around prenominal modifiers. What? You aren't excited about that? (I know, the grammar jargon scares me a little too.)

Fascinating or not, though, knowing where to place—or not place—your commas is important. Imagine the chaos that might ensue if you littered the ground with them. Someone would surely worry that you'd become ill if not a bit disorderly.

When you have multiple adjectives in front of a noun, you separate them by commas, right? Usually. There are a couple exceptions, and size, shape, condition, age, color, origin, and material are among them. Do you remember this exception to the rule when you write?

For example:

- The adorable white cat is in shock.
- His new pink rubber toy boggles his little kitty mind.
- It's so hard to keep his paws on the Italian marble floor, when his two-month-old worldview has just shifted.

Did you catch all of the different uses of commas with adjectives ahead of a noun? Did you notice the lack of commas? There are more details I could discuss concerning cumulative adjectives and coordinate adjectives, but keeping an eye on adjectives of size, shape, condition, age, color, origin, and material is a good start.

Commas are captivating, aren't they? (Oh, there I go making you shake your head again.)

Writing Tip #161: Single vs. Double Quotation Marks

Sometimes, we are so clever we invent grammar rules that don't actually exit. When uninformed web writers also jump on the popular-but-not-actually-correct bandwagon, we're in trouble, so I'm here to set the record straight.

The use of single vs. double quotation marks comes up fairly frequently, and it's a rule that is often confused. But you know what? This answer is easy—so easy in fact that I can write it in nine words:

> *Always use double quotes unless inside of another quote.*

How simple and straightforward is that?

Yes, this means that single words or short phrases need double quotes. Yes, this means you should use double quotes for titles of songs, articles, poems, and short stories.

The only time we Americans should see the single quotation mark is like this:

"The commenters on web message boards might say, 'No way! I don't believe it,' but it's true," the grammarista explained.

Other English-speaking countries have variations on this rule, but for my American readers, let's keep it simple. Follow the above, and you'll always be correct. And who doesn't like always being correct?

Writing Tip #162: Punctuation at the End of Quotations

Punctuation can be a prickly adversary. Add quotation marks into the equation, and some people close their eyes, hit the keyboard, and let commas and exclamation points land wherever gravity compels them. I propose a more planned approach.

- Ending commas and periods are simple.* Unless you're dealing with academic citations, always put them inside the quotation. ("What? That can't be," you say? Indeed, though commonly confused, this is the rule. Really.)
- Ending question marks and exclamation marks require some thought. Is the quotation asking a question or declaring something emphatically, or are you? Or in other words, is the question or excitement in the original quote or is it something added by you as the writer? ("I love grammar!" she bellowed. Did she really say, "I love grammar"?)
- Ending semicolons, colons, dashes, and asterisks are also simple. Always put them outside the quotation. ("Wow"; "wait"; "what's a semicolon?")

*Simplicity varies across oceans. We're discussing American grammar standards here. Rules vary a bit in other English-speaking nations.

Writing Tip #163: Ellipses

You know . . . I think . . . we all are using the ellipsis way too much these days . . . There's a diet I can get behind.

Did you know that ". . ." is called an ellipsis? Did you know that, technically, when you're removing a few words from a sentence, you should use three periods, and if you're omitting a full sentence or more from a quotation, you should use four dots? Or maybe, that's simply for the academics . . .

My note to you: keep your ellipses to a minimum. It's fine for personal correspondence, but don't overdo it . . . especially in business settings. (Sorry, I couldn't resist.)

Writing Tip #164: Apostrophes

Apostrophes are either the confetti of punctuation marks or perhaps the favorite mark of grammarian vandals. They are added to words at random, so I like to tell myself they were put there by either excited little elves or mischievous gremlins. Too much? Maybe. I guess it's simply time to rein in your punctuation, folks.

Let's review the proper usage of apostrophes.

Contractions

If you want to squish some words together, apostrophes are great for that.

- I am becomes "I'm."
- "We will" becomes "We'll."
- "He does not" becomes "He doesn't."

I could go on, but I really don't think I need to.

Possession

We all remember from the time we learned it in elementary school that adding an "–'s" makes something possessive. If your name is Brian, for example, then this is Brian's book. (If you feel like I'm talking down to you, bear with me. It's time to get this one right.)

If the noun you wish to make possessive is plural and ends in an "s," add the apostrophe but no additional "s."

I know you're with me so far, so let's step it up a notch.

What if you have two people and they own something together? Do you know how to handle your apostrophe(s)?

In this case, you might speak of Rachel and Erin's dance party in their room. (Yes, I'm claiming you can own a dance party.) Note how the "–'s" only appears on the final noun in this joint ownership situation.

However, if two people both own different things, the apostrophes need to change. For example, you could write about Lee's and Lisa's dinners that came with a side of fries. These are two different dinners owned by two different people, thus an "–'s" is needed after each name.

Please don't add apostrophes when you are making something plural. And, I suppose that I should remind you that apostrophes are not actually confetti to be tossed about in times of celebration or otherwise.

Writing Tip #165: Apostrophes With Names Ending in "S"

We'll talk about the incorrect use of apostrophes in surnames, when attempting to refer to multiple members of the family in a bit (See Writing Tip #216 for more on this), but this subject of apostrophes (which began in Writing Tip #164) deserves some more attention. Admittedly, there's contention on this one—and we all know to stay away from fanatical grammarians when things get heated—however, I tend to agree with *The Chicago Manual of Style* when it comes to making names that end in "s" possessive.

As we learned early on in our grammar training, when a singular noun becomes possessive, we add an apostrophe "s" onto the end:

- The man's phone
- The book's title

First names are no different.* Yes, even when they end in "s":

- Kris's tips
- Tobias's yo-yo

Because plural nouns only gain an apostrophe when they become possessive, often people add the apostrophe to names ending in "s" in the same form. Yet, say one of the above phrases aloud. You're adding the extra "s" in your head, aren't you?

I want to argue that last names follow the same thought, but I'll admit that this rule seems to be more flexible than that of the first names.

- "The Waters' heirloom" and "the Waters's heirloom" are both acceptable.
- "The Vyas' house" and "the Vyas's house" are both fine.

Keeping things simple is my favorite argument, so I recommend the apostrophe "s," but I'll put my red pen away on this one.

*I hate when rules have exceptions, but there are two to note: Jesus and Moses. Why? I have no idea other than a guess that people don't like to call out flaws in a sacred text. Nevertheless, when you see reference to "Jesus' words" or "Moses' staff," there's no need to call the Pope.

Writing Tip #166: Writing About Decades

The apostrophe. It's the super-size-me of punctuation marks. Who would want a plain word when you could add an apostrophe with that, right? Let's talk about our overpunctuating, folks. We're getting grammatically obese, and it doesn't make any sense.

Sure, we've talked about unnecessary punctuation with "its," "you're," plural names, and more (See Writing Tips #84, #153, #164, #165, and #216). Now let's focus on referencing decades.

The 1980s is the span of years from 1980–1989. If you want to abbreviate it, call it the '80s. There is no possessive apostrophe "s." The 1980's is weird and nonsensical. The 80's is just confused. Please stop writing that. I beg you.

I am a child of the 1980s. The 1990s were my coming-of-age years. Maybe the super-size-me culture started before my time, but let's start declining the extra punctuation now. Tasty as it may be, it's not good for you.

Writing Tip #167: The Em Dash vs. the En Dash

Did you know that there are multiple lengths of dashes and different uses for these lengths? There are three basic marks to be aware of:

- The hyphen (-).
- The en dash (–).
- The em dash (—).

I know, I just blew your mind.

Each of these marks has a different function.

The hyphen connects closely related words, such as "merry-go-round" or a "happy-go-lucky" attitude (more on using hyphens to transform words into adjectives in Writing Tip #169).

The en dash is used with ranges, commonly dates or page numbers, for example, February–November 2013 or pages 2–57. Notice there is a space before and after my use of these dashes. This is present here because 1) certain style guides, such as Associated Press (AP), dictate it to be so, and perhaps more importantly 2) that's how Microsoft Word allows you to make this dash. For those of you not writing press releases, keep in mind most other writing handbooks recommend that you remove these spaces. My recommendation: whichever spacing format you choose, being consistent is essential.

The em dash is used pretty much everywhere else you want to make a dash—adding additional thoughts into sentences in a way similar to parenthesis is one of them. It also is the proper dash to use for interrupted speech in dialogue. For example:

"How are—"

"You've got to be kidding me!"

Note, according to most style books, except the dear old AP beloved by journalists, the em dash has no spaces on either side of it either. You can see by my usage in this tip what my preferred spacing is.

People are very opinionated about dashes in the twenty-first century—not to mention when they're out of season Labor Day—Memorial Day (okay, maybe that last one's a stretch, but I had to get all three forms in there).

Writing Tip #168: Hyphenating Numbers

If you're talking about songs that can most easily stick in my head, have me nodding along twenty-four/seven or at least until it finally leaves me, I'd say my top track is Nena's "Ninety-Nine Red Balloons," or "99 Luftballons" to give the original title. We may be well into the twenty-first century, but if you hum one-tenth of this refrain from more than a decade ago, I'll be lost for hours.

You know what else seems to make people lost for hours? Where to put their hyphens when it comes to numbers. It's really not as complex as it seems.

Remember:

- Hyphenate compound numbers under one hundred, (for example, "ninety-nine red balloons" or "twenty-first century").
- Hyphenate written fractions except when the second portion is already hyphenated ("one-tenth of this refrain," "two-thirds majority," or "one ninety-ninth").

When numbers work together with another word to create an adjective, they should also be hyphenated, but there's more on that in Writing Tip #169.

As for now, who knows a good way to get a song out of my head?

Writing Tip #169: Hyphenating Words Working as Adjectives

We all take artistic liberty with our word usage from time to time, and one way to do so is to make adjectives from words that are not adjectives. It's like magic. Abracadabra and poof, a string of words that used to have other functions are tied together into a new way.

The magic comes from your use of hyphens.

Whenever you merge two or more words before a noun to create a new modifier, these hyphens make the usage of these words clear:

- Black-magic grammarian
- Tip-filled book
- Houdini-style trick
- One-minute confusion
- A quick-thinking apprentice
- A who-done-it mystery
- Top-10 tips
- A nose-in-the-air attitude

Note that normal usage of multiple adjectives or an adverb plus an adjective do not require hyphens. Don't get hyphen-happy, but do be aware of when you need them.

I know magicians shouldn't share their secrets, but when it comes to grammar magic, I think it's okay.

Writing Tip #170: "#-Year-Old" vs. "# Year Old"

Remembering how old you are is one thing. Remembering where to put (or not put) the hyphens when you describe your age is another.

A thirty-four-year-old woman should be able to write grammatically. I am thirty-four years old. A thirty-four-year-old is old enough to know.

Did you see those hyphens (or lack thereof)? They're all correct. Do you know why?

Here's the reminder:

- If the age is being used as an adjective or as a noun (as in my first and third examples), use hyphens.
- If the age is part of the adjective phrase following the noun (as in my second example), don't use hyphens.

When a child is two years old, he or she doesn't care about grammar. Maybe a ninety-year-old still doesn't. Either way, though, knowing the rule doesn't hurt.

Idioms

There are phrases that are so interwoven into our everyday lives that we don't often take the time to consider them. These are the expressions that, although not always logical, we have heard since our earliest days as English language speakers. But the problem with phrases that are a part of our spoken vernacular is that often, when we try to spell these idioms, we don't always record them as they should be. Furthermore, for those who are speakers of English as a second, third, or fourth language, these phrases can be a matter of utter confusion.

Maybe you've heard of "eggcorns," a funny term that refers to words or phrases that people write incorrectly from how they hear it said. "Eggcorn" itself comes from a common confusion with the word "acorn" long ago. Say the word. Let it roll off your tongue and out of your lips, and you'll hear an accent that makes this confusion completely understandable. And there are a lot of eggcorns in the world of idioms.

The following list of 17 is only the beginning.

Writing Tip #171: "All of the Sudden" vs. "All of a Sudden"

Although Shakespeare often gets credit for creating the idiom "all of a sudden," his contribution might have merely been the addition of the word "all." The usage of "of a sudden" as a synonym for "suddenly" was common in his era.

Thus, the correct wording of this idiom, as it has been for a few hundred years, is "all of a sudden."

There's no logic really between the use of "a" versus "the"; however, there is logic with using the recognized expression rather than a version commonly considered wrong.

Writing Tip #172: "By Accident" vs. "On Accident"

It's a debate for the ages. Seriously, some argue the correct answer depends largely on your year of birth.

Although "by accident" is the standard form, there seems to have been a defining mass-media moment that affected the younger generations. Parallel in form to "on purpose," "on accident" has become common in recent years. The best research breakdown I've seen notes that people born before 1971 say "by accident," that people born between 1971 and 1996 say both forms, and that people born since 1996 say "on accident." Personally, I feel like the youngest demographic of this study might still be practicing their grammar, so I don't give their choice a lot of weight yet. Of course, this could just be a matter of time. As for those of us in the 1971 to 1996 crowd, I think we need to up our game a bit. Personally, I'm all for tradition.

"By accident" is the correct form, and we should all start sticking to it.

Writing Tip #173 "By and Large" vs. "By in Large"

It always amazes me how many of our everyday idioms come from sailing short-hand. We don't live in a highly nautical culture in the twenty-first century, but it takes some sailing-savvy explanations to understand the origins of "by and large," the correct form of this idiom.

Its meaning of "in general" comes from the idea of a wide range, specifically from sailing into the wind as closely as possible and sailing with the wind behind you. Without getting too technical into sailor-speak such as "close-hauled" and "abaft the beam," these sailing directions were referred in shorthand as "by" and "large." Thus, "by and large," entered our general vocabulary.

When you hear this phrase spoken quickly, I understand the confusion with "by in large," but when you're writing, make sure you get it right.

Writing Tip #174: "Case in Point" vs. "Case and Point"

If you want to point to a specific case or example to illustrate your argument, use "case in point," not "case and point."

"Case in point" has been used since as far back as the mid-1700s, but "in point" was a common English turn-of-phrase that dates back to the mid-1600s. Today, its only major remnant is in this idiom.

If you're trying to defend a position, messy word choice can weaken any argument. Use "case in point" to remain on the top of your debating game.

Writing Tip #175: "Deep-Seated" vs. "Deep Seeded"

No matter how much the weather makes you feel like gardening (or perhaps not), there is nothing tracing back to seeds, roots, or things buried far within the dirt with this idiom.

If you have a belief that is held deep in your core, it is "deep-seated"—as in seated deeply within your heart. (Note, there's a hyphen present because these two words are combining to become an adjective. See more on this in Writing Tip #169.)

You don't want to bury your seeds too deeply, or they won't grow. The same goes for this idiom. No more deep seeding, everyone. "Deep-seated" is the way to go.

Writing Tip #176: "Doing a 180" (Not a "360")

When someone makes a drastic direction change, they are not turning in a full circle. If you miswrite this common phrase as "doing a 360" or "pulling a 360," you would be discussing metaphorically going 360 degrees around to face in the exact same direction—turning in a circle, which is 360 degrees.

To turn and go the opposite direction, either physically or metaphorically, you would turn 180 degrees.

Tap into those old geometry recollections and remember what you heard there—it was more than just the squeaky leather shoes of your teacher. Now let that basic math knowledge wash over your writing, and you'll be all the better for it.

Writing Tip #177: "Down the Pike" vs. "Down the Pipe" vs. "In the Pipeline"

Here's another often confused idiom. Is it coming "down the pike" or "down the pipe"? Both have their logical arguments. Something could travel through a pipe toward you (for example, water through pipes, emerging via a spigot), or something could travel along a pike—that is, once you realize what a pike is. It's this latter word that is possibly the source of confusion.

Remember, the correct phrase is "down the pike."

If something is coming "down the pike," it is going to happen or going to appear soon. A "pike" in this sense is an abbreviated form of "turnpike." Here's some trivia for you: did you know that this term originally meant tollbooth? Now, of course, "turnpike" usually refers to the road itself.

And whereas the first piece of confusion with "down the pike" vs. "down the pipe" is the meaning of the word "pike," the second is the separate idiom, "in the pipeline." If something is "in the pipeline," this means that it is in the works or being developed.

Down the pike. In the pipeline. I completely understand where the chaos sets in. Let's look at them in action for one last reminder:

Q: So what's coming down the pike with my writing and editing blog?

A: I have many more tips in the pipeline for you.

Yes, these idioms are so close that they're asking for confusion, but I have faith you can get them right.

Writing Tip #178: "For All Intents and Purposes" vs. "For All Intensive Purposes"

He was Henry the eighth, he was. Henry the eighth, he was, he was.

Did you know that the origin of this tricky idiom goes back to a single member of English royalty? You can blame this phrase on Henry VIII. Its first recorded use appears to be a 1539 proclamation of parliament. And yes, it was written "for all intents and purposes," not "intensive purposes."

As you know, "for all intents and purposes" means for all practical reasons or, simply, in effect.

If you were first introduced to this phrase in spoken English rather than written English, I can understand the confusion, but be sure not to sound silly if you use the expression yourself. For all intents and purposes, "intents and purposes" is the way to go.

Writing Tip #179: "Fowl Swoop" vs. "Foul Swoop" vs. "Fell Swoop"

Perhaps with birds of prey, you might have a "fowl swoop." Perhaps with gangly young basketball players, you might have a "foul swoop." But when you're looking for what to call a sudden, swift action, "fell swoop" is the correct form. How many of you are writing this one right?

You can blame Shakespeare for the confusion. His use of "fell swoop" utilizes an old form of "fell," which means savage or ruthless (as in "felony"), but the exact line in Macbeth where he uses it does also mention chickens. Fell. Fowl. Writer foul?

Of course, fans of the Philadelphia Eagles football team might also talk of a fowl named Swoop, their eagle mascot, but that doesn't make their use of the expression any more correct.

Writing Tip #180: "I Couldn't Care Less" vs. "I Could Care Less"

Hint: if you're talking to a writer or editor, even on social media, try hard to get this phrase right. Heck, if you're talking to anyone, it's worth knowing the difference.

If you couldn't care less about something, that means that you already care so little about the subject that it's impossible for you to be interested in it even less than you already are. I couldn't care less about calculus. Or glittering vampires. Or most forms of reality TV. (Sorry, but it's true.)

If you could care less about something, then that means that you do indeed care about it. You maybe aren't singing it from the rooftops, but there's room for less interest. And maybe you are singing it from the rooftops; that's possible too.

This is a writing and speaking tip really. You need to start getting it right, folks. I'd say I couldn't care less if you do, but I do. I really, really do.

Writing Tip #181: "In the Throes" vs. "In the Throws"

If you're a sports scout or a fantasy football aficionado, you can dissect the throwing arms of players and perhaps use the phrasing "in the throws"; however, if neither of those descriptions fit you, you'll want to stick with the common usage of this phrase.

"In the throes" means to be in a stage of difficulty or suffering.

When referring to someone being "in the last death throes" of something, we're not talking about a quarterback's last Hail Mary before being cut from the roster. The correct wording is to be in the "death throes" or "final throes," which means the last stages, usually when these last stages are rough.

Sure, "throes" isn't a word you use every day, but when you have a moment of glory and get to throw down a rare word, make sure you do it right. And then, feel free to do a touchdown dance, of course.

Writing Tip #182: "Low and Behold" vs. "Lo and Behold"

When you're telling a story and want to express your surprise and excitement, you might insert a "holy smokes," "hot dog," or "hallelujah." There's always "by George," "bingo," or "bazingo." When you want to say it with nineteenth-century style, though, perhaps the phrase you're looking for is "lo and behold."

There should not be a "w" on the "lo" in this exclamation. For example:

- I looked everywhere, but then lo and behold, my glasses were sitting on top of my head.
- I went into the cellar, and lo and behold, there were jars of pickles enough to feed a village.
- I used to use more modern expressions, but lo and behold, I just discovered the fun of "lo and behold."

Whether it's used in a character's dialogue or in your own writing, if you're a bit of a character, "lo and behold" needs to be spelled correctly. Make sure you do.

Writing Tip #183: "One and the Same" vs. "One in the Same"

It's hard to explain how "one in the same" could logically be the correct usage of this idiom unless it's somehow referencing *matryoshka* dolls, or nesting dolls, where one is inside of another that is (nearly) the same as the first, down and down, along the beautifully hand-crafted line. Idioms do come from all over the world, but this one doesn't require any explanations in line with these small wooden dolls.

"One and the same" is the correct form of this idiom, meaning that something or someone is one and not two things or people. It's an expression of redundancy (see Writing Tip #116 for clarification), but that's never stopped a good idiom before. It is one, and it is the same.

Let's take a look at this phrase in action:

- Her coach and her mother were one and the same. (Meaning: her coach was also her mother.)
- Her college entrance essay and her latest diary entry were one and the same. (Meaning: there was only one text written. Oy. Good luck with that.)
- Her favorite season and her most common method of downhill skiing were one and the same. (Meaning: fall. Bad joke. Poor girl.)

One in the same is simply another eggcorn. Don't let your ear trick you. Make sure you have it right.

Writing Tip #184: "Piece of Mind" vs. "Peace of Mind"

If you want to give someone a piece of your mind, it's clear you don't have peace of mind. These are two different idioms with two different meanings, so be cautious with your spelling with them.

We all remember that:

- "Peace" relates to a state of tranquility, and
- "Piece" is a part of something.

Thus:

- "Peace of mind" is a state of inner tranquility; there is no turmoil in your mind;
- "Piece of [your] mind" is an idiom most commonly expressed, "giving a piece of your mind," meaning to tell someone directly about your frustration or anger, usually because that person is perceived to be in the wrong.

Personally, I have no peace of mind when it comes to these two expressions because I see them confused for one another commonly enough. Don't make me have to give you a piece of my mind. Get these idioms right, and we'll all be in a more peaceful place.

Writing Tip #185: "Shoe-in" vs. "Shoo-in"

Are we talking about wedging a foot into a doorway or about shooing something in a certain direction? Do you know?

When this expression is spelled wrong, it's almost justifiable. To "get a foot in the door" is a common idiom, and this one could be related . . . but it's not.

"Shoo-in" is the correct form, first appearing in the early twentieth century in regards to horse-racing. A horse was a "shoo-in" if it was a "sure thing."

If you remember the old song "Shoo, Fly, Don't Bother Me," you can understand this use of "shoo." You want to shoo a fly away from your picnic. However, you could also shoo it toward something. Shoo it toward the finish line perhaps? This may not be a common case with flies, but with horses, politicians, and so much more, being a "shoo-in" is a familiar turn of phrase.

Maybe you don't write "shoo-in" often, but when you do, make sure you leave your footwear out of it.

Writing Tip #186: "Slight of Hand" vs. "Sleight of Hand"

Maybe you have a love of magic. Maybe you had that uncle who always pulled a coin from your ear. Maybe you always cheat at cards (shame on you). Whatever the case, make sure you're writing the correct idiom.

"Sleight of hand" is the correct way to write this phrase. The word "sleight" doesn't get much use these days, but it means dexterity or cunning.

If you were writing about "slight of hand," then that would refer to small or feeble hands, but I don't think that's what you're aiming for.

Writing Tip #187: "Wreak" vs. "Wreck" Havoc

Pronouncing this phrase, there isn't often confusion, but when it comes to writing "wreak havoc," fingers somehow tend to get confused as they type away on their keyboards. Has this happened to you? If so, here's a gentle reminder:

- To "wreak" means to inflict or create; thus, to "wreak havoc" means to create havoc or to create chaos or mayhem.
- If you're "wrecking havoc," you're truly a force to be reckoned with because you're destroying chaos. Watch out for you. I know I will.

Watch your spelling, and make sure you know what you're saying, folks. Throwing a hashtag in front of "havoc" isn't enough to save you.

Business Writing and Etiquette

Writing more formally isn't a matter of being false or faking it. It's a matter of respect.

Understanding who will be reading your words is essential in communicating successfully, and in a business atmosphere, professional success is exactly what is at stake.

There's a Portuguese expression, *Quem não se comunica se trumbica*, which translates literally as "He who doesn't communicate gets his fingers burnt." This idea is a metaphor about getting into trouble when you don't express yourself well, but sometimes, in the business world, it really can feel like your fingers are getting burnt. Maybe it's a missed job opportunity or a passed-over promotion. Maybe it's a typo that cost a business deal or a client's high regard of your work.

Writing appropriately may seem at times superficial, but how is one to understand who you are, the work ethic you have, and the attention to detail that you can tackle if your messages are muddled?

As you have no doubt noticed, I don't always write formally. In fact, I break a number of the rules in this section through the course of this book. However, there is a time and a place to putting on that power suit and that confident, take-charge attitude. When you go to the office, you dress to impress. Your words in this environment should be no different.

Writing Tip #188: Avoiding Jargon

Sometimes, we become so immersed in the language of our industry or our discipline that when we try to communicate with people outside of our sphere, a communication roadblock appears. We are convinced we are being as clear as we possibly could be, but we're speaking in an entirely different language without realizing it. This is the language of jargon, or the vocabulary of a specialized trade, industry, or group.

If you're in the accounting department, feel free to talk about receivables, accrual, and remuneration all you want to with your peers, but when you're creating a report for your board, skip the lingo.

Our goal with all writing is to make ourselves understood and to make it as easy on the reader as possible. Confusing your audience or giving them the homework of deciphering your language is the exact opposite of this objective.

Honestly, avoiding jargon is the goal of this book. Sure a few "misplaced modifiers," "appositives," and "infinitives" have slipped in, but in each case, I try to make my writing as clear as possible. Don't intentionally or accidentally intimidate, segregate, or shamelessly show off your smarts. Be inclusive. It's true for being a good person and being a good writer alike. Your readers, whoever they may be, will appreciate it.

Writing Tip #189: "Conversating" vs. "Conversing"

I don't quite know where this word arose, whether it was in the late 90s or somewhere long, long before, but I suppose its origins don't matter. What does matter is that "conversating" is not a word.

- "Conversation" is the noun form.
- "Conversing" is the verb form.

You don't sound smarter using a long word if the long word is imaginary. If you do use this term, the concept of you being smarter will be imaginary too. And that's something to avoid, isn't it?

Writing Tip #190: The Necessity of Clarity

Have you ever tried to explain something in the simplest terms possible, but somehow, in the process of things, written yourself into circles around the idea, like a vulture circling its prey but not quite landing, like a lasso twirling in the air not yet catching anything, and whether it's your wordiness, punctuation blunders, or lack of clarity in your own head, a single sentence becomes muddled and unnecessarily befuddling?

Whoa, let me shake myself off and try that again. (All writers have to do that sometimes, you know.)

Being clear is important. It's vital that we understand what we are trying to say before we attempt to say it, and once we do understand exactly what we are trying to communicate, we need to do so in the sharpest way possible.

Does this mean that we should edit ourselves after we spit out our first draft onto our paper or screens? You betcha.

Does "editing" mean diagramming every sentence and pulling out red pens to painfully tattoo our text? Not at all.

Here's my recommendation: before you press "send" on that email or "print" on that report, step away for a moment. This can be done with a walk down to the water cooler or simply by closing the active window on your screen to focus on something else for five minutes. Even this short break will allow you to see your words anew. It will enable you to catch yourself if something might come across less than polite or terribly mistyped, but above all, you can reread your writing to see if what you intended to say is actually being said. Is it clear? If it isn't, there's no point to that communication at all.

There's a place for a long, winding sentence that moves a reader from idea to idea like a line of falling dominoes. A corporate communication, however, is not that place.

Writing Tip #191: Familiar Abbreviations Only

You know who knows a lot about VCIN and NCIN? Virginia-based police officers and 911 dispatchers do. These acronyms stand for the Virginia Criminal Information Network and the National Crime Information Center respectively. Dedicating one's professional life to trying to help the greater community is admirable. Knowing when to use the abbreviations of your industry, such as these, and when to avoid them in communications with non-insiders is almost equally so.

I'm not simply focusing on the police force. Every industry has their lingo. We've discussed jargon in Writing Tip #188, but abbreviations needed their own spotlight.

If you're in the tech industry and you're writing about SERPs, SEO, and WYSIWYGs with others who understand what you're talking about, that's absolutely fine; however, if you're trying to create marketing materials for general audiences, you need to take a step back.

When we are so immersed in our work, abbreviations sometimes roll off of our tongues and our fingertips onto the keyboard without a second thought; however, we always need to consider our audience first. Is the communication an interdepartmental email, where everyone included speaks the same language? If so, use as many acronyms as you'd like. However, if the communication is external—be it to customers, business partners, the media, or your mom—show a little respect and take a step back. Explain your point in laymen's terms so no follow-up questions are needed.

Everyone will appreciate it.

Writing Tip #192: "His" or "Her" vs. "Their"

When discussing pronouns, there's a larger conversation to be addressed that you might not have seen coming. There's a linguistic debate that's been intensifying with every year that goes by. It's been going on for centuries, and recently, it has become even more heated. Jane Austen and the King James Bible both have their stance, and it may surprise you which direction they often choose.

There was a moment in history where grammarians declared that the singular pronoun "he" should be the automatic stand-in when the gender of someone is unknown. For example, "A child will fall if he doesn't tie his shoes." If this is a generic child and this is a reminder written for all parents and children, the male singular form was the norm. This was also the same era that utilized "mankind" and "men" in reference to all people. Whether used for the sake of simplicity or as an example of the larger male-dominated society is a matter for another conversation that needs space more than this single writing tip allows, but in short, if you're pondering your pronoun options, I recommend against utilizing the male-only form.

As equality of the sexes became more of a conversation in society, pronoun recommendations evolved too. The sentence, "A child will fall if he doesn't tie his shoes," became, "A child will fall if he or she doesn't tie his or her shoes." The logic argued that if one doesn't know the gender of a subject, one should not always assume male.

The problem many find with this "his or her" construction is that it quickly becomes wordy. For example, "A child will fall and hurt himself or herself if he or she doesn't tie his or her shoes" is a bit of a linguistic mess. Yikes. There's being politically correct, and then there's being unnecessarily longwinded.

In addition, the LGBT community argues that "he" and "she" isn't inclusive of all people. Other pronouns have been suggested from "per" and "pers" to "xe," "xem," and "xyr" to "ve," "ver," and "vis"; however, my argument—an argument that both Jane Austen and the King James Bible agree with—is that the singular use of "they" has its moments.

- A person needs to remember to tie their shoes.
- Somebody should put it on their to-do list if they cannot remember.
- No one likes it when their shoelaces have been dragged through puddles.
- The applicant, Jessie, turned in their resume.

"Person," "somebody," and "no one" are all regarded as singular, but using "they" with these word choices can work fine. Moreover, if an identity is unclear, be it a gender neutral name or otherwise, that "they" covers all of your bases.

If you're not convinced, let me point you to two formidable references who agree with this point.

In Jane Austen's *Pride and Prejudice*, Elizabeth Bennet says to Mr. Darcy, "To be sure, you knew no actual good of me—but nobody thinks of that when they fall in love." This is hardly the only use of the singular "they" for Austen. It's a form she favors.

In Matthew 18:35, the King James Bible says, "So likewise shall my heavenly Father do also unto you, if ye from your hearts forgive not every one his brother their trespasses." And again, this singular "they" appears multiple times throughout this translation.

Personally, I feel like these two sources hold some weight for the singular "they."

It comes down to what is more important to you? Is it accuracy of gender or accuracy of number? Yes, there is a degree of political correctness and human equality as a part of this conversation, but, I argue, what's wrong with that? Isn't having a simple answer preferred to potential confusion or offense?

Writing Tip #193: "Kind of," "Sort of," and Other Vague Descriptors

When you write, you want to create yourself as a knowledgeable authority, not a waffling push-over. You might not realize it, but every time you insert these little hesitancies like "kind of" and "sort of," your position becomes a tad weaker.

Maybe you're inserting these words because you feel like they make an order or a request kinder. Maybe you're inserting them to ease a complaint or accusation. Maybe you don't realize that they are as common in your speech and written communications as they are.

Do you see the difference between "I kind of didn't like it when you said that," versus "I didn't like it when you said that"? The latter has more confidence behind it.

Do you see the difference between "The project you delivered was somewhat disappointing" versus "The project you delivered was disappointing"? There's more authority in the second example.

Do you see the difference between "The requirements for the proposal were kind of confusing" versus "The requirements for the proposal were confusing"? In the first, the confusion comes from the writer's competency, and in the second, the requirements are more at fault.

Try to strike all of the following from your business communications:

- Kind of
- Sort of
- A bit
- Somewhat
- In a way
- Pretty much
- Slightly

Whether it's subconscious or intentional, these words show your hesitancy. You can be better than that. You know it. Now it's time to display that competency and confidence to everyone who reads your work.

Writing Tip #194: "In Lieu of" vs. "In Light of"

In light of the state of written communications today, I decided to write this book in lieu of pursuing a career as an acrobat. Would I have made an awesome addition to Cirque du Soleil? Probably not. But either way, I think writing this book was the better choice—for me, for the English language writing crowd, and for audiences of acrobatic shows worldwide.

- "In lieu of" means instead of or in place of. It came to English in the late thirteenth century from the Old French term *lieu*, also written as *leu*, which meant position, place, or situation. Thus, "in lieu of" became "in the position of" or "in the situation of," just as we use it today.
- "In light of" means considering or in view of. It's been used this way since the 1680s.

Yes, they are both phrases that start "in l-," but is that enough to cause the confusion? There's no muddle between these words and "in latkes" or "in lightning," after all.

So in light of my affinity for words and language, I wanted to tackle a project to be helpful to the masses. In lieu of a pursuit of gymnastic ability, a mastery in latke cooking, or dancing in lightning, this is the path I have taken.

In light of this tip, you'll never confuse "in lieu of" and "in light of" again, will you?

Writing Tip #195: The Value of Being Concise

Truman Capote once said, "I believe more in the scissors than I do in the pencil." Upon first glance, these words might make you do a double-take. He was a great writer, after all. How could the cutting of words be more valuable than the act of putting them down? Yet in my opinion—and Capote's as well apparently—it's this finely trimmed examination that makes any message as brilliant as it could be. It's the difference between having a communication that's long and shaggy and one that looks ready for school picture day.

No matter what you're writing, every sentence needs to carry its weight. Furthermore, every word you choose in that sentence needs to be necessary. If you are too verbose, you can lose your readers because of length alone.

When you have a point to make, in business communications especially, simply say it. Make sure it's understandable and written with respect, and then move on.

I discuss this in more detail in other tips, such as Writing Tip #193: "Kind of," "Sort of," and Other Vague Descriptors; Writing Tip #196: Unnecessary Transition Words; Writing Tip #197: Cutting "Just"; Writing Tip #198: "Actually," "Basically," and Other Filler Words; and Writing Tip #199: "I guess," "I suppose," and Other Hesitations; among others, but for the moment, I believe I've said all I need to on this subject. Because that's being concise. Boom.

Writing Tip #196: Unnecessary Transition Words

I feel a bit self-conscious in writing this tip, but I have to call myself out as a bad example. As you've noted from the tone of this book, I enjoy writing in a casual style. Being playful, relaxed, and a tad rebellious is fun; however, the buck stops here (or some other stern, serious-minded expression).

When you are writing for business, you must always remember that you are writing for business. Resumes, reports, and emails to supervisors should be composed with the proper levels of respect, decorum, and succinctness, but above all one's tone needs to be professional.

One of the quickest ways to lose this professional tone is in one's transitions.

Just as written dialogue for a short story needs to capture the natural ebb and flow of conversation minus the everyday small talk, business writing needs to cut the casual insertions common in everyday speech.

Examples of transition words that should be cut from business writing include:

- Well
- So
- Oh yeah
- Okay, so
- Yeah, and
- Anyway
- Anyways (see Writing Tip #20)

In place of these words, learn to use gems like:

- However
- Moreover
- Likewise

- Speaking of which
- Nevertheless
- Conversely
- In light of
- In lieu of (see Writing Tip #194 for more on these last two)

These aren't clichés of corporate-speak. They demonstrate capable organizational skills and a mastery of professional communication.

Think about the difference in a composition that segues using the first set of phrases compared to the second. Who do you imagine as the writer of the first versus the second? Which category do you want yourself to be a part of within the business world?

There is a time and a place for the casual voice; however, when corresponding with professionals, your tone needs to be stepped up a notch. You don't wear your flip-flops to a board meeting (I hope), and your writing needs to be dressed up to match your business attire. Elevating your transitions is often the easiest first step to transitioning your writing to something more acceptable for this new audience.

Just wait to see where it will take you.

Writing Tip #197: Cutting "Just"

I just wanted to let you know that I have something to say about this. Wait, did that come off a bit weak and hesitant? Aren't those two traits you don't want to show off in your professional life?

The word "just" is another example of a word we slip into communications when we don't want to be too forceful; however, rather than softening a message, it often softens your authority and expertise.

Don't start a message, "I just wanted to reach out" or a similar phrasing, because isn't it clear that by sitting down to write a message, you clearly wanted to reach out?

Don't start a message, "I was just thinking" or a similar phrasing, because if you want to look like you're good at your job, I sure hope you were thinking and that you still are.

Don't add "just so you're aware," because hopefully the person reading the message understands that you are writing to tell them something to be aware of. This phrase adds nothing.

"Just" is often a filler word that can be cut with no loss and often a major gain of authority. Striking it adds to your strength and confidence and also makes your message more concise. What's not to love about that?

Writing Tip #198: "Actually," "Basically," and Other Filler Words

I actually see these filler words all the time. Basically, they add little to a sentence. They're much like an "um" or "uh" in spoken language, where someone pauses to collect their thoughts before continuing. A solid presenter learns to pause without making these verbal grunts, and a strong writer needs to learn to cut this filler as well.

Words in this filler category include:

- Actually
- Basically
- Literally
- Just about
- Honestly

If you want to step up your communications a degree further, you could even cut some of these filler phrases:

- I think that (it's clear you are thinking if you are composing a message about something).
- I believe (again, this is clear if you're sharing your ideas).

- What I'm trying to say is (no need to hesitate, get to the point).
- To be honest (I sure hope you're being honest).
- To make myself clear (if you strive for clarity, you don't need this line).

These aren't words that weaken your expertise like those vague descriptors discussed in Writing Tip #193, and they aren't words that lessen your authority like "just," as discussed in Writing Tip #197. These filler words simply slow down the point that you're trying to make. You can do better.

Writing Tip #199: "I Guess," "I Suppose," and Other Hesitations

Imagine beginning a message that shares a new idea: "I guess my idea for the solution is . . . " How much confidence do you see in these words? They're not quite dripping with it, are they? In fact, they don't seem to have much conviction at all. No matter how brilliant the idea, it might not win over the board of directors.

The same hesitancy shows up with other beginnings:

- I suppose
- I think
- I believe
- I wonder
- I figure
- I imagine
- I reckon

Others that potentially could have the same downfall include

- I find
- I assume

- I presume
- I suspect
- I expect

Beyond the unnecessary focus on "I" (more on this in Writing Tip #203), many of these introductions have a degree of doubt to them. Perhaps you don't want to come on too strong with a concept that will redefine an event or reimagine a long-standing practice, but you don't want to present any ideas without your full self-assurance behind them either.

These are not all phrases to avoid in all situations, but "I guess," "I suppose," and other hesitations should make you pause before finalizing your communication. Are they adding anything to your message? Are they making it unnecessarily wordy? Are they undermining your authority?

Sure, everyone you work with might not always show you your due respect, but your own words shouldn't be the ones holding you back.

Writing Tip #200: Cutting "In the Process of"

Four words you can almost always cut with no loss to the whole are "in the process of." She's in the process of folding a paper airplane. He's in the process of tweaking his design. I'm in the process of launching mine to see how many cubicles it can cross. All these little four words are really saying is that something is happening at this moment. You know what else says the same thing? The use of the present tense.

Why tell your boss that you're "in the process of checking up on something," when you can simply say you're "checking up on something"? Why tell your colleague that you're "in the process of studying for your certification," when you can more easily say you're "studying for your certification"?

Utilizing "in the process of" has a wordiness similar to that of "try and" or "try to" ahead of an update of your actions. Writing that you're trying to study for your certification is no better than being in the process of studying. (Of course, see Writing Tip #139 for more on that pair.) These are all unnecessary words and phrases that can be cut to make your writing more concise, sleek, and aerodynamic.

Well, maybe not aerodynamic, but if you're really good at paper airplanes and your boss is a bit of a free spirit, maybe it's not a bad idea for interoffice messaging. There's little threat of hacking. And cutting "in the process of" will make your message shorter, thus keeping it down to potentially one page. Everyone will have to work on their aim, though. I suppose this would be slightly more hazardous than the click of a send button.

Writing Tip #201: Communicating With Respect

When you were a child, did you learn to address your elders with "yes, ma'am" and "yes, sir"? Were you instructed to look someone in the eye when you spoke to them and to give a firm handshake? Did a parental figure ever tell you, "if you don't have something nice to say, don't say anything at all"? Okay, maybe that last one came from Thumper's mom in Walt Disney's *Bambi*, but it's good advice all the same. These ideas are powerful when it comes to respecting others in person, but we all have to remember to show the same respect with our written words.

How do we show respect with our communications?

- Begin correspondence with the name of who you are connecting with. This simple step may seem formal, but it begins any conversation in a considerate manner.
- In an opening correspondence, take a moment to be personable. This does not necessarily need to be your opening sentence—in fact, moving this line or two of relationship building to the end of your message can allow you to state your purpose and end on a friendly note—however, taking

a moment to focus on something other than the task at hand establishes an accessible tone.

- Utilize "I" sentences or "We" sentences instead of "You" sentences in moments of disagreement or dispute. There's something much nicer about "We misunderstood each other" or "I'm not comfortable with this" than "You are wrong" or "You are an idiot."

- Avoid words that are judgmental. No matter how much you want to call someone's actions or behavior "childish," "daft," "thoughtless," "asinine," or a similar less-than-kind word, take a moment to ask yourself whether this will add anything to the communication. These words are likely fueled by your emotions, and they will only make a conversation less productive. Hold back, writers, even when it's hard.

- Be clear on what you're trying to say. (Refer back to Writing Tip #190 for more on this.)

When you are less than thoughtful about your communications, you can put others in a defensive mode—whether you meant to be offensive or not. Remember, being respectful doesn't mean losing your own voice or being subservient. It means communicating with others to show that you see them as equals. Their rank may be higher or lower than yours, and your personal opinion of them could be wonderful or terrible; however, that's no reason to be anything but polite.

Respectful communication boosts morale and potentially increases productivity because everyone feels valued and appreciated. It can feel forced sometimes, but the end result will nearly always be the better for it.

Writing Tip #202: Cutting the CAPS

When you need to stress a point, there are many ways to do so. You can utilize bold, italics, or an underline, of course. You can break out a bullet point or numbered list, which can be highly effective in laying out specifics in an easily digestible manner. Some people even highlight a particularly important phrase. Yet of all the options you have, avoid WRITING IN ALL CAPS.

Writing in all CAPs isn't perceived as emphasis. It's perceived as yelling. CAPs come across angry, like the schoolyard bully who isn't getting enough attention. They're standing up tall and trying to be intimidating, but often they're more distracting than anything else. Most people react to that schoolyard bully by either puffing up their own chest defensively or feeling a bit wounded and shrinking away.

Are these the reactions you want your employees to have? Is this the tone you want to bring to a conversation with your boss?

Headlines and graphics might use CAPs in a design layout, but when it comes to everyday communications, lift your sticky finger from the shift key or caps lock button. You will have a better response if you communicate with respect, even if the matter is urgent, even if you are angry, even if you were oblivious to the tone of this formatting change.

In my opinion, bold, italics, underlines, and any of these formatting changes should be used sparingly, of course. In many situations, focusing on your language is enough—your words can say what you mean rather than a font change. (Mind-blowing, I know.) It's a bit of a communication challenge, really. Can you make your message clear with your words alone? Go on, I dare you.

I DARE YOU. Just kidding. (But ooh, wasn't that intense?)

Writing Tip #203: Moving Beyond "I"

One of people's favorite words in the English language is their own name. When we speak or correspond with someone else, using their name makes that conversation more personable. It makes it clear that the speaker or the writer is indeed focused on the person and conversation at hand.

Talking about me, me, me often has the opposite effect. It's true for dating, and it's true for writing. The problem is that we often don't realize that we're doing it.

For example, think of the following communication:

Hi team,

I hope everyone's having a great day.

I was thinking about the project we were discussing, and I had an idea. I used to do projects like this, and I found that I liked it when I was able to use my expertise . . .

Sometimes we don't realize how often we use the word "I" in our communications. Before you press send on your next email, double-check yourself. How many times do you use "I"? Are you accidentally making yourself sound self-centered?

Explore how you can rearrange your lines to focus slightly less on yourself. It's good advice for dating and writing alike.

Writing Tip #204: Double-Checking the Spelling of Names

You always want to start a correspondence off on the right foot, and the quickest way to lose the reader of your communication is by misspelling his or her name. If you clearly aren't taking the time to get someone's name right, then how much attention to detail will you give moving forward?

Whether it's a first name or a last name, writing the incorrect "Mr.," "Mrs.," "Ms.," or "Dr.," "Lady," or "Lord," these things matter.

Double-checking names is a mandatory element to any editing process. Of course, you should do a thorough editing of your entire written text; however, if nothing else, make sure you spell someone's name correctly.

What is a rose by any other name, after all? A rosé perhaps. A Rosie?

Whatever it may be, it's something of extreme value—something you cannot ignore.

Writing Tip #205: Avoiding Red Font

This is a topic that makes some scream, "yes!" and others raise their eyebrows and say, "buck up, softies!" No matter which one of these responses is your gut reaction, avoiding red font is a writing recommendation not to be ignored.

There are two major reasons I recommend against red font:

- First, just like writing in ALL CAPS, words in red font are often understood as reprimands or angry in tone. Think of the meanest teacher you ever had as a kid and the red ink smeared like blood across the papers you brought home. Now that you feel all warm-and-fuzzy with that memory, imagine spreading that love with the readers of your words. (Please, please note my sarcasm.)
- Second, font should never be highlighted by only color because roughly 8 percent of the male population is color-blind. The percentage of color-blindness in women is significantly lower, but also notable. Therefore, if you are using text of any color to stress information, this stress will potentially be missed by a lot of people.

If you need to emphasize one or more of your words, using bold, italics, an underline, or a similar font option will be significantly clearer and less offensive.

Avoiding a red font can also be important for signage in the sun. For example, I once saw outdoor signage that read "Alcoholic Beverages Prohibited Beyond This Point," where the word "Prohibited" was in red. However, after some time outside, that red word was only visible if the reader was really close. Thus, from far away, it red "Alcoholic Beverages Beyond This Point." For a moment, it seemed there was probably a pretty good time on the other side of that fence. I wonder how many others read it and wanted to go join the party.

Whether you are choosing a color for your hyperlinks on your website or distinguishing important deadlines in a work memo, be careful with your red font, everyone. Sun-fading aside, it can get you into trouble.

Writing Tip #206: Elevating One's Language

There's the way you can speak to your old college roommate whom you have known for twenty years and then there's the way you should speak in a job interview. Depending on your personality, these voices could be very similar or worlds apart. The key is knowing what is appropriate for either situation. Knowing your audience for your writing is equally important.

As a teenage girl in the 1990s, I was told that my generation overused the word "like." And, like, you know what? This word isn't the only culprit. There are a lot of these transition and filler words that slip into writing that make people look as unprofessional as Cher from *Clueless* (for more on this, see Writing Tips #196 and #198). Furthermore, the use of casual or slang speech can lessen your professionalism and your expertise in the eyes of others, no matter how knowledgeable you may be on any given subject (see Writing Tip #207 for more discussion of this area).

Sometimes we get too excited about ellipses (see Writing Tip #163); sometimes we develop a pattern that makes it look as if we don't know what a complete sentence is; sometimes it's a use of contractions in academic essays or more formal reports when the full word should be used.

Well, you know, I mean, so . . . yes, it's true. Be on guard. On social media or in a chat with that old college roommate, it's one thing, but when sending an email to your boss, it might, like, you know, look bad. Avoid the "facepalm" or worse yet, the "headdesk." Step it up a notch, writers.

Writing Tip #207: Avoiding Slang and Nonstandard English

This writing tip shouldn't need to be written, but sometimes people forget—or worse yet, they don't even realize that they're doing it.

We live in a verbal culture, and people write more today than perhaps ever before. That being the case, knowing your audience is essential. Telling your employer that you need to "bail" on a meeting—even if it is for the best of reasons—says something about your professionalism (or lack thereof).

If the data that comes in from Q3 is a bit astonishing, don't end your report with "for real."

Don't apologize for "screwing up." Apologize for making a mistake.

And OMG, beware of Internet-inspired acronyms. There's a time and place for them, but the workplace isn't it.

Beyond slang and other overly casual phrasing, also be careful not to slip into nonstandard English in a professional setting. I'm not talking about perfecting your "who" and "whom" choices; I mean, avoid words and phrasings that some might consider incorrect. Examples of this could be "would of" or "woulda" instead of "would have," "yous" instead of "you," "let's us" instead of "let us," "hisself" instead of "himself," and so many more.

Flipping the switch on your writing from everyday communication to a more formal style sometimes feels forced, and it often takes practice. However, your professional life will thank you. With strong communication skills in your toolkit, who knows where you will go and what you will do next?

Writing Tip #208: Avoiding Generalizations

When political candidates or cocktail party guests refer to all (insert group of people here), I generally stop listening. Whether they're talking about all men, all Southerners, all lawyers, all people of a certain background, or otherwise, when you put all of any given population into a box, it usually ends up as a blanket statement, a generalization, that I'm not comfortable with.

How can I not be comfortable with a blanket statement, you ask? Doesn't that sound pretty cozy? Don't be fooled by terminology. A generalization is a statement about a group of people or things that doesn't allow for exceptions. They are often inferred from a small amount of information or research.

Let's look at some examples of generalizations in action:

- "Everyone knows that Thanksgiving is the fourth Thursday in November." (Although this writer assumes this is common knowledge, the word "everyone" implies every single person knows this. It's a bit much to presume, even when something seems obvious.)
- "English majors are dull." (Every single English major in history? Really? I'll try not to take offense to this, but my bigger issue is the clear lack of consideration. There are always exceptions, aren't there?)
- "The weather is always better in Florida." (Always, eh? Do you think the same thing during hurricane season? It's not so true then, is it?)

In casual conversation, these statements seem like moments of hyperbole for effect, but when you're writing, especially in the business world, you want to appear like you know what you're talking about. A generalization may appear like a gaping hole in your reasoning, exposing your lack of consideration for other ideas. Whether it's an essay for class, an argument in court, a debate about a new product or service offering, or a note to your sweetheart about dinner plans, you look more intelligent when you aren't throwing out sentences that are little considered.

Writing Tip #209: "First" vs. "Firstly"

Yes, I understand what you're thinking when you're starting off a list "firstly." You're thinking an adverb makes sense there, just like "moreover" or "conversely." However—ooh, look another adverb—there are a few problems with "firstly," not the least of which are the words that come after it. Sure, "secondly" and "thirdly" aren't that bad, but what about when you get up to "fourthly," "fifthly," and "sixthly." It doesn't quite roll off the tongue (or the pen), does it? There is formal writing and then there is writing that overthinks a concept, and that is exactly what "firstly" and its numerical buddies are. The grammatical rule to remember when this internal linguistic struggle comes up is that "first" can act as an adjective or as an adverb.

I know you're saying "wow," and wow is right. These are the grammar epiphanies that change our writing. Think about the following usages:

- She was the first in her class to learn number writing rules. ("First" is an adjective in this case. It modifies "she.")
- She learned number writing rules first and then went out for recess. ("First" is an adverb in this case. It modifies "learned" and speaks to when and how she learned them.)

Therefore, if "first" can be both an adjective and an adverb, that silly "firstly" can be tossed aside and forgotten like past centuries' usages of "shall" versus "will." It's a bit superfluous, turning a word that can be an adverb into an adverb. It's like giving Superman an extra cape. It really doesn't add anything to his identity, does it?

In close relation to "first" and "firstly" are "in the first place" and "at first."

- "In the first place" is a wordy way to say "first."
- "At first" refers to time, meaning at the beginning.

These are the lessons that might not be first and foremost in your writing education, but they sure do help along the way.

Writing Tip #210: Misleading Quotation Marks

Quotation marks never create emphasis. They only cause confusion. Are you using yours properly?

It makes me smile every time I see bungled quotation marks on store signage, business marketing materials, or even in personal communications. Please don't continue this downward trend. If you want to emphasize your language, use bold, italics, an underline, or even surround something with *asterisks* if you must, but do not—I beg you—use quotation marks.

Besides where to put them around other punctuation and when to use single versus double quotes (See Writing Tips #161 and #162 for more on this subject), here's what you need to know about quotation marks:

- They surround exact words that someone said or wrote.
- They surround a title of a song, poem, or article.
- They surround a word that is being defined or discussed.

That's roughly it.

If you are trying to use quotation marks for emphasis, you will miss. Instead, your words will be understood as sarcastic, ironic, euphemistic, or deceptive. And is that really what you wanted to say about your "free" cupcakes? Suddenly those delicious treats became a tad sketchy. What do I have to do for those cupcakes, really?

I know this punctuation blunder is a huge pet peeve for a lot of people. You may not even realize that what you're doing is wrong, but moving forward, try to remember.

Writing Tip #211: "Centered Around" vs. "Centered On"

Where is the center? In the middle, right? So how can the center be around something? Aren't these two concepts a bit of an oxymoron when placed next to each other? You're either at the center or you're around. Will everyone please stop saying and writing "centered around" now?

If you really feel the word "around" calling to you, try out "revolve around" instead. Maybe it will make you feel better.

"Centered on" is the proper phrase. This is so at least in American English. Oddly, in other parts of the world "centre on" and "centre around" have become largely interchangeable—though "centre on" is still regarded as the proper form of the phrase. But note the spelling change of "centre" in these cases. Unless you're spelling it like the Brits, stick to "center on."

It's rare the Americans are the stricter grammarians, isn't it?

Writing Tip #212: "Flesh Out" vs. "Flush Out"

If you're trying to flush out an idea, are you trying to scare it out of hiding? Is that really what you mean? Maybe in some sort of complex psychotherapy that is beyond me, this makes sense, but I'm guessing that wasn't what you were going for.

- "To flush out" is an expression that originates in bird hunting. Perhaps dogs could help flush out the quail to get them to leave their hiding spaces.
- "To flesh out" means to give substance to. If you had a skeleton of an idea, you could flesh it out to give it weight.

Personally, I smile every time I see people writing that they are "flushing out" their thinking. Our ideas can be sly sometimes, I suppose. We have to get at them however we can. Who am I to judge?

Just make sure you know what you're saying.

Writing Tip #213: "Internet" vs. "Web"

Let me reintroduce you to these two words, "Internet" and "Web." People use them like they're synonyms, but they aren't actually. I want to explain and save you the embarrassment of being called out on this by some techie wearing a snarky T-shirt.

- The Internet is a global network of computers, which was built as a decentralized grid with no central hub. Some examples of how the Internet is used today include the World Wide Web, email, VoIP (voice-over IP), Internet-based security systems, and IoT (Internet of Things) devices.
- The Web, shorthand for the World Wide Web, exists on the Internet, but it is only one piece of the whole. Think of the "www" in front of domain names when you are in a web browser. The websites you visit and the pages you can discover via a search engine and via hyperlinks are all on the Web.

The Internet has its origins in the 1960s. The Web was launched to the public in the early 1990s. Debates continue on the capitalization of the words "Internet" and "Web." At this time, stylebooks vary in their answers.

Writing Tip #214: "Login" vs. "Log-in" vs. "Log in"

Here's an interesting case of computer programming influencing spelling. Have you ever noticed the difference between "login," "log in," and "log-in"?

Although some argue that "login" is never correct—that it should either be "log-in" or "log in"—the use of "login" is growing. Why? There are a few possible arguments. Some argue "login" is becoming common because spaces are not used within coding languages, and hyphens can be read as a break between two separate words. Others argue that "login" looks cleaner from a web design standpoint. Either way, when these rules trickle into the nondigital world, grammar chaos ensues!

Getting back to the correct, original usage of these words:

- To "log in" or "log on" to a site (log in/log on as a verb), you should always use two words.
- If you ask a user for their "log-in" information (used as an adjective) or simply for their "log-in" (noun), the hyphenated form is correct.

The hyphenated form is often where the one word "login" is used interchangeably, but you know there's a heated grammarian hullabaloo about this. (Oh, the many ways you can annoy a grammar stickler . . .)

Writing Tip #215: "Online" vs. "On-line"

There is a trend that new terms often begin as two words (for example, "electronic mail") evolve into a hyphenated form ("e-mail"), and then finally are accepted and commonly used as a single word ("email"). "Online"—yes, one word—has a similar story.

Style books have evolved on matters of "e-mail," "e-commerce," "web-site," and "on-line" as these terms have become a part of our everyday lives. Capitalization is lost, and hyphens are thrown out with yesterday's floppy disks. Now, "email," "ecommerce," "website," and "online" are the recommended forms of these words.

Unless you're still printing your words on your dot matrix printer, I highly suggest you follow suit.

Writing Tip #216: Family Names

No matter how many times you see it printed on invitations, cute beach bags, and graceful signage by the front door, apostrophes never make a family name plural. Never. Retailers sometimes seem convinced of the opposite, but it isn't true.

Apostrophes should only be used to indicate possession or a contraction. Don't use them incorrectly, referring to a family as the Jones' or similar. Add "s" or "es" to refer to a family group, never an apostrophe.

Example 1: Happy New Year from the Smith's! (Incorrect. Unless this is from the Smith's dog or pet chinchilla, "Smiths" is the proper form.)

Example 2: Happy Nothing Day from the Smiths! (Correct. And who knew there was such a thing as "Nothing Day" every January 16th?)

If the family name ends in an "s," then you would add an "es" to make it plural.

Example 3: Happy New Year from the Floreses! (Correct.)

Example 4: Happy National Grammar Day from the Floreseseses (Incorrect. You may be taking this too far.)

Be careful with your embroidery, everyone.

Writing Tip #217: In-laws Plural

When you visit your extended family, are you sure of how to refer to everyone? No, I'm not talking about your second cousin through marriage once removed who always makes you feel bad because she clearly remembers your name. I'm simply talking plurals. Is it sister-in-laws or sisters-in-law?

Much like the tricky plural of passer-by, the "s" is added onto the first word in the sequence, the central noun "sister" in this case.

Sisters-in-law, brothers-in-law, mothers-in-law, fathers-in-law— it's a diverse world; the possibilities are endless. Just make sure your grammar doesn't turn anyone against you.

Writing Tip #218: Capitalizing Seasons

Shall I compare thee to a summer's day? No, I'm not talking about springtime in the mid-Atlantic coast. Have you ever been confused about when to capitalize the names of seasons?

A lot of people think that seasons are like proper names and that, therefore, they must all be capitalized. These people are incorrect in their assumptions.

Unless a season is named at the start of a sentence or is part of a proper name, you don't need to capitalize it. I know you want to fight me on this one, but it's okay. Take my hand. Don't hit that shift button. It can simply be spring, summer, autumn, or winter. No capital letters required.

Writing Tip #219: "Biannual" vs. "Biennial" vs. "Semiannual"

Do you know the difference between "semiannual" and "biannual"? Or is there a difference? What about "biennial"? (Cue the *Jeopardy* music.)

This is another one that trips up native speakers. A lot of folks don't realize that "biannual" and "biennial" are two different words with two different meanings. Sure, they both start with the same "bi-" prefix, referring to two of something—like a "bicycle" with two wheels or a "bipod" with two legs—but we all see that the rest of these words are not spelled the same.

Remember:

- "Biannual" means to happen twice a year.
- "Biennial" means to happen once every two years.
- "Semiannual" is interchangeable with "biannual," also meaning to happen twice a year. This word, of course, uses the different prefix of "semi-" which denotes a half, like "semicircle," which is half of a circle, or "semi-truck" which is a truck whose trailer cannot move without the other half (the engine).

Some people like to keep it safe and avoid confusion by staying away from "biannual" altogether.

I knew one writer who kept this straight by remembering Victoria's Secret has a semiannual sale. What business would survive off a big sale every two years? Throw in supermodels in their underwear and maybe Victoria's Secret would do just fine, but that's beside the point, right?

Writing Tip #220: "Regard" vs. "Regards"

Regarding "regards" or "regard," remember that the singular form of "regard" is proper in phrases such as "with regard to," "in regard to," and similar forms. This seems to be a loose rule these days because it's found incorrect so often—even in edited material—but if you're looking for a straight right-and-wrong answer, there you go.

The plural form of "regards," is correct in signatures and sign-offs, such as "best regards" or "warmest regards." It's also the proper form when you're "giving your regards"—to Broadway or anyone else.

Writing Tip #221: "Regardless" vs. "Irregardless"

"Irregardless" is not a word. Please stop using it. Don't you love it when things are simple?

Creative Writing and Storytelling

Since the earliest days of humankind, we have been storytellers. Capturing tales of wonder and woe, history and humanity, fear and fascination is an art—it always has been and it always will be.

We tell stories in fiction, in nonfiction, for the stage, for the screen, in poems, in prose, and in advertising campaigns. Yet one idea that often escapes people regarding the creative arts is that they take practice. One might have a natural inclination toward writing and storytelling, but only by exercising the skill will one become a master—if a form of art can be mastered at all.

There might be early stories that will stay in your drawer forever; there might be rough drafts that are as hideous as any monster of your nightmares; there might be the creation of an absolute gem that redefines how you think about your writing life.

Athletes have the ability to train together. For writers, this is sometimes more difficult. But you must keep training, keep learning, keep finessing your lines, cajoling your characters, and brushing the dust off of your words until they are as spotless as they can be. And if the following 29 tips help your process, all the better.

Writing Tip #222: Cutting Unnecessary Adverbs

Adverbs can make even the most brilliant writer sloppy. They're the litter of the parts of speech. They might serve a function in some places or for a short period, but in the end, they often need to be thrown away. Don't let your workspace be littered with balled up sheets of paper, and don't let your story be littered with adverbs.

These little words are often examples of where you are cheating as a writer. Don't write that a character is speaking happily. Show your reader that happiness in how he moves, the words he uses, or in how he sees the world around him. Don't write that a character walked softly. Say that she tip-toed. Don't write that the tree is extremely big. Instead, tell us that it is enormous or colossal. Better yet, how could you evoke the weight and grandeur of that size in the eyes of your characters?

I'm not talking about writing adverbs in first drafts. In early versions of a story, adverbs can litter your pages where they may, but when you're in the refining stage, seek them out. You'll find that the trashcan is where most belong.

If you're unsure, ask yourself:

- What is this adverb adding? How could I evoke this in another way? Through action? Through atmosphere? Through the character's dialogue?
- Is this word even necessary? Does it add anything to the whole? Is the action, atmosphere, or dialogue already making the point, and thus this word is redundant?

Pro Tip

When your manuscript is in digital form, do a search of your entire story for "ly." No, I don't mean doing it page by page manually. We have tools for such things. Use "Ctrl" + "F" to search your entire document, and your pesky adverbs will be handed to you on a digital silver platter. Then one by one, you can decide whether it stays, goes, or can be refashioned into something better.

For those who think a search for "ly" is too cumbersome, because it will also turn up words like "fly" and "lymphoma," feel free to search for "ly " (do you see the extra space there?), "ly," (the comma should be part of the search), and "ly." (again, the period as part of the search).

Searches like these won't catch every adverb, because they don't all end in "ly," of course; however, you will be shocked at how many times your characters might speak "softly" in moments of suspense or how they will do things "slowly" when they are being thoughtful. Sure, an occasional adverb isn't the death of a manuscript, but you can do so much better than the adverb litterbug style we all have been known to slip into.

Writing Tip #223: Empowering Every Sentence (i.e., Not Starting With "It Was . . . ")

Not since "It was a dark and stormy night," has "It was . . ." been a recommended start to a sentence. And, really—if we're getting down to it—the famous Edward Bulwer-Lytton quote could have been stepped up a notch.

Think about the difference between "it was a dark and stormy night" and "the stormy night was dark." The switch is a simple one, but suddenly, the line is more direct and a bit ominous.

A writer could (and should) take it further, practicing the old advice of "show, don't tell" (more on this in Writing Tip #226). This exercise might lead to a more evocative sentence still: "The storm crashed through the night, blackening the lights in the windows of the few night-owls that remained." Do you see how this line doesn't simply use the adjectives "dark" and "stormy"? It builds an image for the reader.

And as I'll discuss more in Writing Tip #230, when it comes to building images, the more specific, the better.

When you start a sentence with "it was," do you even know what this "it" stands for? If you don't know, you can do better.

Before you finalize any project—be it a manuscript, an essay, a business document, or dare I say a social media post—do a quick search for the phrase "it was." Nine times out of 10, you can rewrite these weak lines with something more powerful.

Writing Tip #224: The Thing About "Thing"

The word "thing" is the word that you use when you can't remember the actual word that you need. It's true, isn't it? "Thing" is up there with "stuff," "what's-his-name," "whozits," "whatsits," "thingamabobs," and "snarfblats"—okay, maybe not that last one. Anyone else have a song from *The Little Mermaid* pop into their head? No? Yeah, me either.

Admit it. We're not always the best communicators. Sometimes, we form sloppy habits without realizing it. On this note, edit the word "thing" out of your writing whenever possible. I promise: you can find a better word. Whether writing professionally in the corporate world or taking on a more creative project, this is one word you shouldn't allow yourself to use. Take it up as your own challenge. Unless you learned your vocabulary from a seagull named Scuttle, you can do so much better.

Writing Tip #225: Crafting a Character's Body, Mind, and Soul

You know what's great about people? We're all different. How I say something is different from how my neighbor would, which is different from how my mom would, which is different from how a small child would. Why? We're different people. We have different language patterns, different brains, and different life experiences.

Moreover, if you put me in a room with these people, the way I stand—perhaps with my hands hooked in my pockets—is different from my neighbor who might be stretching after an intense workout, or my mom who might be stirring something on the stovetop, or a two-year-old who, well, has an inability to stand still.

People are different. When you write about your characters, allow them to be distinctive. All shouldn't wink at each other when they say something clever; they shouldn't all gesture with their hands, nor sigh heavily, nor twirl their dark mustaches menacingly (okay, maybe you weren't using that last one for everyone). When writing falls into a pattern, you see the author's personality, not the characters'. The author should be the invisible hand that guides the story, not the center focus.

Think about body language differences, speech patterns, and movements between personalities. Everyone has their own mannerisms, nervous tics, excited habits, angry habits, and so on. This is a great way to tell more about your characters, while showing their different emotions (more on this in Writing Tip #226, momentarily). It takes some practice, but it makes for better writing.

––––––––––

Writing Tip #226: Show, Don't Tell and What it Actually Means

Every writer who's ever taken a creative writing class has heard the instruction: "Show, don't tell." It's so often said, it's almost meaningless—except it shouldn't be. If truly understood, being able to show and not tell can make the difference between a humdrum story and a tale that comes alive.

"Show, don't tell" is classic writing advice, and for good reason. Imagine the difference between reading, "she's angry," and reading, "her hands tightened into fists; her fingernails pressed so hard against her palms that blood surfaced to her sensitive skin." You see what I'm going for. There can be a named emotion, and then there can be the reality of it that a reader can be pulled into.

Let your readers see, hear, feel, and smell what's going on. Like a movie, let them take in the entire scene. You cheat them when you briefly summarize. Don't say the room was small; make your reader feel claustrophobic. Don't say a character is tired; show the weight of his day on his motions and his mind. Let your reader live through the scenes with your characters, being made to feel what the characters feel, seeing them move through vividly created places and react as people, not as two-dimensional, flat beings.

Imagining themselves fully in your world, your readers will become more attached, and getting your readers attached to your characters and your world is the entire point.

Writing Tip #227: Sticking to One Point of View

Choosing the right point of view (p.o.v.) for a story is hard. Sticking to that point of view can be even harder. This is a lesson that applies to creative writers, sure, but it's also important for anyone trying to tell a story—be it in the voice of a brand, the voice of a pirate ghost trying to protect its lost treasure, or otherwise.

The key is consistency. Whatever narrative voice an author chooses, they must stay with it through the course of their text. Website homepages cannot jump from first person plural (we) to third person (the Acme Company) within a paragraph, and novels cannot vary between third person omniscient and third person limited (with rare exceptions). When the p.o.v. isn't stable, the story becomes a bit wobbly—and not just for the picky editors among us.

What are your point of view choices?

First person singular: Writing in the voice of "I," relating ideas from your own (or a character's own) perspective. This is the most personal p.o.v., allowing a reader into one's world. Hint: First person narrators are unable to share the thoughts of other people or actions that occur when they aren't present unless this information is learned in a clear way.

First person plural: Writing in the voice of "we," relating ideas from your own group or business, speaking on behalf of multiple people. It's as personal as first person singular, but more community-based.

Second person: Writing directly to your audience, utilizing "you." This p.o.v. can be powerful for a brand, but can be challenging in fiction (though do-able).

Third person limited: Writing as an outsider looking in, utilizing "he," "she," "it," and "they," but focusing on one character. The narrator would know the thoughts going through perhaps the protagonist's head, but would not be able to know or share what others are thinking. Hint: You can convey the thoughts and emotions of others by showing, not telling (see Writing Tip #226). Third person limited can allow for an intimacy with a character that can be similar to what can be achieved with first person singular.

Third person objective: Writing as an outsider looking in, utilizing "he," "she," "it," and "they," but only sharing observable information. This means not explicitly noting anyone's thoughts or intentions. Hint: Again, a skilled writer can show, not tell, where all is still clear.

Third person omniscient: Writing as an outsider looking in, utilizing "he," "she," "it," and "they," but with everything known and knowable. In fiction, this means everyone's thoughts, history, and actions are able to be on the page for your readers; however, beware of losing focus with this point of view. Interesting tangents not directly related to your main story line can be distracting. You may have access to everything, but that doesn't mean that you should tell your readers every tiny detail that goes into your world.

Be thoughtful with your writing, folks. It takes a lot to tell a powerful story, and point of view is a big decision in the process. Once you've found the voice that suits you, make sure to stick with it through the very end. Your readers (and editors) will thank you.

Writing Tip #228: Cutting Sensory Verbs in Description

When we have a clear image of a place or a moment in our heads as writers and we want to convey this picture to our readers, multiple challenges arise. How long should our descriptions be? How do we make sure our description doesn't kill the momentum of the story? How much is too much? What should we leave up to our readers' imaginations?

Yet in all of the questions about description, one stylistic choice can dramatically improve the end result: cut the sensory verbs that introduce your description.

Let's take a look at two examples to showcase my point.

Example 1: He saw the vulture fly over the woods and circle back, and he heard movement in the brush below. Johnny was still and waited. He smelled the pine needs of the loblollies and felt the wind with the cool hint of coming rain.

Sure, it's not terrible. A scene is being shared with readers, and multiple senses are included, which always makes a description more vivid (see more on this in Writing Tip #229). However, do you see a difference when we strike all of the sensory verbs (that is, "saw," "heard," "smelled," and "felt")?

Example 2: The vulture flew over the woods and circled back, and movement jarred the leaves in the brush below. Johnny was still and waited, surrounded by the smell of pine needles from the tall loblollies. The cool wind hinting of rain blew on his skin, giving him goose bumps.

Often, we use our characters as stand-ins, letting our readers imagine themselves in these different shoes. Yet when we always introduce our descriptions with these sensory verbs (he saw/heard/felt/smelled/tasted), the effect is weakened. We're reminded of a character rather than the place and moment we're trying hard to describe. Momentum is slowed because of wordiness.

Whether you're writing fiction or nonfiction, examine your descriptions closely. Are you using sensory verbs as unnecessary filler? Why waste time on unnecessary introductions when you have the chance to simply make the story come alive?

Writing Tip #229: Description via All Senses

When writers show readers the world around their characters, imaginations come to life. Readers are transported from their easy chairs into the woods at Red Riding Hood's side, the depths of the ocean with Captain Nemo, or wherever you as the writer decide to take them.

We often think about the visual when we think of description, but writers shouldn't be limited to what they can see. Sounds and smells can add richness to a scene, as can the way something feels. Taste is a bit less common, but it can be powerful in the right context.

There's a difference between Anna walking into a bakery and Anna walking into a room where flour and sugar danced like dust in the air, covering every surface, including her lips with a sweet note of birthday cake.

There's a difference between Yuki standing on the street and Yuki standing on the street, surrounded by the rattles of jackhammers, and the smell of the dumpster full of rotting produce wafting out of the alleyway behind him.

There's a difference between Ira stepping into the woods and Ira stepping into the woods, feet sinking into the squishy moss, skin moistened by the mist from the crashing waterfall.

You don't have to use every sense in every moment, but the more you can weave into your story, the more your readers will be able to step out of their world and into yours.

Writing Tip #230: The Power of Specificity

It's all in the details, folks. As writers we know this. We want to make scenes real for our readers, but we have to be specific and often unique in how we do this. It's hard to visualize "outside," but if you introduce your readers to the splintered garden fence, the singing chickadee with its black hooded head, the wind with a hint of springtime's warmth, and the smell of the compost pile for the next season's carrot planting, a more complete picture is presented.

Specifics are important. Unique details are important. Don't describe a cliché scene everyone has seen so many times before. Create a place that is distinctive, a place that is only yours for only your readers. It's not easy. It takes time. But the payoff is readers who will always come back for more.

Writing Tip #231: New Paragraphs With New Speakers

If you were writing a screenplay or a play for the stage, you would know that before each character speaks you note their name ahead of their lines. Other creative pieces aren't as clear cut when it comes to dialogue, but what they do have in common is that each speaker begins their words on a new line.

For example, note the following conversation:

"I have this awesome idea for a new story."

"Oh, yeah? What's that?"

"It involves a love triangle between robots and takes place in a dystopian near-future where a reincarnated Alexander the Great is trying to save the world."

"Um, that's . . . interesting."

"Isn't it, though?"

Did you catch that I didn't have a single dialogue tag, noting who was saying what, but you could stay with the conversation, because every time the conversation switched to a new speaker, the text on the page followed suit with a new paragraph?

Don't forget this simple formatting. Your story is much more likely to find readers if you make it easy on them and follow the basic rules of dialogue structure.

Writing Tip #232: Dialogue Tags

We talk to people all the time. We listen and interact, because that's what people do. Then why is it that writing dialogue can be so tricky?

I've discussed the power of using dialogue to differentiate characters (see Writing Tip #225) and will shortly discuss not overusing character names (see Writing Tip #242), but now, let's focus on dialogue tags, the "he said," "she said," or similar phrases surrounding a character's spoken words.

Three Tips for Stronger Dialogue Tags

- Dialogue tags are only necessary when the reader is unsure who is speaking. It's often stronger and tighter to skip unnecessary tags through dialogue that rings true to specific characters and your other narration.
- Keeping it simple is often the best way to go. Using "said," "asked," and comparable words isn't necessarily dull. Dialogue tags are there to serve a purpose. When you get too colorful with your tags—"bellowing," "wailing," or "thundering," for example—it distracts from the story. (Meanwhile, adverbs surrounding dialogue tags are another conversation entirely. For more on this, see Writing Tip #222.)

- Allow the dialogue to remain the focus by inserting dialogue tags (if needed) after a character's words. Writing "he said, 'the sky is falling'" puts the focus on "he" rather than what's being said. Reversing it and writing "'The sky is falling,' he said" keeps the focus on the story. Of course, the format of inserting dialogue tags within a character's words—such as "'The sky is falling,' he said. 'Watch out!'"—is also a strong option.

Dialogue can sometimes feel like we're transcribing the voices in our heads, and sometimes it feels pulled out of our characters with difficulty; however, in the midst of a story, don't let the dialogue tags be what holds anything back.

Writing Tip 232.1

"Dialogue" is the more commonly accepted spelling of words spoken in a literary form; "dialog" is most commonly used in computing (for example, dialog boxes).

Writing Tip #233: Thinking to Oneself

Why is it that people so often write that someone "thought to himself/herself"? Is there a way to think to anyone outside of oneself? If so, can you teach me? That would be pretty cool.

My advice is to cut the useless words and keep it simple—no more of this "to myself/himself/herself" prolixity. Until science enables alternatives with telepathy or otherwise, the clarification is pointless. Just think your thunk. The world will understand it's an internal process.

Writing Tip #234: Smiling and Overused Body Languages

Some stories have happy endings. Others just have happy. So much happy. Happy that drips from their pages in a less than helpful way. Are your characters smiling perhaps a bit too much?

The root of all this happy is coming from a good place. People realize that they need to not just say characters are happy, but they need to show that happiness in action. The problem is that writers need to think beyond the smile. Yes, it is a simple way to show happiness, but characters fall a bit flat if they are smiling all the time about everything. Maybe it's a shy smile. Maybe it's an excited smile. Maybe it's a smile with lips pressed together trying to hold back a laugh that's trying to escape.

People are different, and their smiles should be too. Beyond that, how can you think beyond the smile? How can you show friendly without writing about a smile? How can you show delighted? How can you show love?

Writers have an endless vocabulary at their fingertips if they only press themselves a tad harder than the first word that comes to their mind.

Personally, I love smiling, but this action is overdone in early drafts of manuscripts.

Search for it amid your pages. Use "Ctrl" + "F" to seek out "smil"—yes, that spelling is intentional. Searching for "smil" will catch "smiling," "smile," "smiled," "smiley," and who knows what else you've stuck in there.

A smile or two are fine, but please don't overdo it. Unless you're writing another *Stepford Wives* and you want that happiness to feel a bit false, be cautious. Evoke cheerfulness; don't make your pages feel repetitive. Plus, when you're more original, that will make your readers happy.

Writing Tip #235: Where to Start Your Story (Not With Waking Up)

Just because a character's day starts with his or her morning routine doesn't mean your chapter needs to start there too. We all wake up in the morning, put on our clothes, brush our teeth, and eat our breakfast. Sometimes we stretch. Sometimes we yawn. Do you see how fascinating this paragraph is? Wait, it's not? I'm glad you're noticing, because this is exactly my point.

People don't want to read about everyday details. As writers, we get to create people and worlds and plots. We get to stir ideas and distract readers from their everyday. So why give them more of the everyday?

Creative writing can have so much potential. Every page, every paragraph, every sentence, and even every word should drive the story forward. If a character is wiggling his or her toes under the blanket, opening his or her eyes, and seeing the sun break through the window, a reader isn't being pulled in. Ask yourself, how can you intrigue the reader? The morning Cheerios aren't doing it.

Writing Tip #236: Stop Looking in the Mirror

Mirror, mirror, on the wall, what's a way to describe your characters that's cliché above all?

There are many ways to detail your characters' appearance, but there are a number of ways we have seen so often that they have turned into clichés. Writing in clichés is often a way to have readers, literary agents, and publishers close your story because they've seen it before (more on this in Writing Tip #241). And that's the last thing you want to happen, isn't it?

To have your character look in a mirror and then detail what they see—eye color, hair color, skin tone, height, weight, clothing, etc.—has been done. It's been done to death. It's probably even been done to zombie characters at this point, which would literally be done to death itself.

The same cliché holds for gazing into reflections in ponds, reflections in window panes, and reflections in soup spoons. Remember, your readers don't need a paragraph of head-to-toe physical description. You can weave what they need to know into the story.

Breaking mirrors may lead to bad luck, but cutting them from your stories will only help your cause.

Writing Tip #237: It Isn't All a Dream

The Wizard of Oz is an awesome story. There's good and evil and a girl on a mission. There's singing scarecrows, some rocking red shoes, and flying monkeys. Flying monkeys, people! What isn't awesome about flying monkeys? In addition, when we get to the end of the story and Dorothy wakes up back in Kansas, audiences are left wondering, was it really all a dream? Did it all really happen and waking up was a part of the magic that brought her back? L. Frank Baum's story is a classic, but it is one of many stories that accidentally started a revolution in a cliché ending.

The Wizard of Oz was first published in 1900. A lot of time has passed since then. Today, readers often feel cheated when the explanation they meet on the last page is that the entire story that they have been pulled into was simply a dream by a character tucked cozily into his or her bed.

This isn't only my pet peeve. Publishing industry professionals speak openly about the dreaming cliché that many writers use to wrap up their stories. It may make for a tidy ending, but you don't want your conclusion to be a letdown. Shouldn't it be as original as the rest of your story?

As a further note, crafting a wild story that ends up all being a dream is a similarly cliché move for the first chapter of a book. It's been done so many times that it's no longer clever. The start of a story is where you are pulling the reader in, connecting them with your characters and your world. Don't create a disappointment so early on. A lot of people might not continue after this point.

In short, please stop dreaming, folks. Wake up, and see what original brilliance you can unfold.

Writing Tip #238: Avoiding "Suddenly"

You suddenly have this idea for a great story. You pick up your pen, when suddenly the phone rings. It's your publisher who suddenly has had this brilliant idea about your marketing campaign that can turn your manuscript into the next bestseller.

Is this awesome? Parts of it are, definitely, but parts of it aren't. There's that pesky word "suddenly" stuck in a bit too often. Does it increase the pacing? Perhaps. Does it quickly become stale and a bit contrived? Absolutely. Don't let the overuse of "suddenly" weaken your storytelling. Allow your vividly crafted scenes to keep your readers on the edge of their seats, not an overused writing trick.

There are many words we write into our stories, and I've already named a number that exist perhaps too much on our pages. The word "suddenly" is another. Seek it out (using that handy "Ctrl" + "F" trick I've mentioned), and cut it where you can.

Writing Tip #239: Avoiding "Then"

There was a chase. And then the good guy jumped over the fence, and then the bad guy saw the gate unlocked and ran through it after her (What? Who says the "good guy" can't be a girl?). Then he caught up to her and grabbed her arm. Then she unleashed her inner woman warrior she'd tapped into in a recent self-defense class. He gasped and then groaned as he fell to the ground.

You know what's wrong with this scene? Sure, many things, but one was exaggerated to make a point. We are overusing the word "then," people!

Is any meaning lost between the sentences "he ran; he jumped" and "he ran; then he jumped"? No sense of timing is missing when the word "then" is cut.

I feel like we sometimes use "then" in our creative writing to intensify the suspense and pacing of a scene, but really, it makes the lines clunky and wordy—the exact opposite of our stated goal.

When you are finished with your next writing project, why not utilize that ever handy "find" feature (Ctrl +F) and seek out the word "then." How many did you write? How many can you cut? How much better will your story be because of it?

Writing Tip #240: Writing Out Laughter

Before the era of emoticons, writers established a bad habit of spelling out their laughter reactions in emails, text messages, social media posts, and beyond. Gushing over a cute boy at a coffee shop? Tee hee hee. Guffawing over a well-placed verbal jab? Ha! Scheming a maniacal plan to take over the world? Mwahaha.

The problem is that this spills over into prose, and we need to nip that in the bud.

Spelling out your characters' laughs in many ways returns to the same "show vs. tell" conversation we've had before (see Writing Tip #226). You want your readers to be so immersed in your story that the laughing flows naturally in their ears. The moment a writer takes the time to spell it out, a reader can be pulled out of the story. Maybe they heard it differently in their minds; maybe they would have spelled it using different letters; maybe it's too gosh darn silly looking sitting there on the page.

This isn't a matter of "literature" versus other writing. This is a matter of not distracting from the story you're telling. It's a matter of evoking emotional energy in a scene and not talking down to your readers.

In all honestly, there might be one person who can get away with spelled out laughter. Who would Santa Claus be without his "Ho Ho Ho"? However, if you're not writing about the jolly old elf, please break the spelling-out-laughter habit in your stories.

Your writing might be a laugh a minute, but we don't need to see it quite so clearly.

Writing Tip #241: Avoiding Clichés

Writers, it's time to think outside the box and stop using phrases like "think outside the box." Why would you choose to tell your story using the same plot lines and turns of phrase that you have read countless times before? Originality is what defines a writer's voice and pulls in readers. When you write using too many clichés, you aren't giving yourself a chance to shine.

Don't say a comment "sliced to the heart of the matter," that a character is "cute as a button," or that a moment "made his hair stand up on end." Push yourself to avoid weather that "rains cats and dogs," a character that "is coming down the home stretch," and a race that is "neck and neck."

Of course, clichés can go beyond word choice and into your character, plot, and setting.

If you're writing horror, for example, please don't have your beautiful heroine trip on her stilettos when the monster is right behind her.

If you're writing about a sleepy southern town, go for it, but find a way to make it come alive in your readers' minds as a place they've never seen before. You need more than gatherings on front porches with sweet tea in hand and rockers outside the general store.

Sure some plot devices and character types are tried and true, but there's a fine line between genre expectations and something so formulaic that it's been overdone.

If you're unsure of the originality of an idea, challenge yourself to try something new. Sure, this isn't something that you need to work on when you're fleshing out your rough first draft, but when it comes to the later polishing stages, pay attention to your clichés. Often, they slip into our prose without us ever realizing it.

A word to the wise, go back to the drawing board. The devil is in the details. Catch my drift?

Writing Tip #242: Overusing Names

Reader, you know what comes across a bit strange?

What is it, Kris?

Well, reader, have you ever read something where the characters use each other's names way too often?

I don't know what you mean, Kris.

Wow, part of me cringed writing that. Do you see what I'm going for? Sometimes, newer writers have this tendency. Rather than making the language unique or the characters alive through their behaviors, names are dropped way more often than is natural in a normal conversation.

Pay attention when you speak with others. How often do you use names? How often do other people? Use real life as your guide, dear reader. Otherwise, reader, it comes off a bit forced. Don't you think, reader?

Writing Tip #243: Repetitive Words

Did you know that the first known use of an ampersand (&) was found within anonymous graffiti on a wall in Pompeii?

"Anonymous graffiti on a wall in Pompeii?"

First things first, yes, this is true. Second, do you overuse repetition in dialogue to stress important or interesting moments?

"Maybe," you say. "Maybe, just maybe, I do."

I'm not sure quite where this started, but I see it in manuscripts of newer writers often enough that I need to make a point of it. Sometimes, it is a repetition of a revelation, and sometimes it is a repetition of a word or phrase within a line.

Perhaps if the echo was a verbal tic that belonged to one character, it could make sense, but if multiple characters follow this pattern, you're showing your readers the writer's voice, not your many characters' varied voices. In addition, it feels a bit contrived. These wordy repetitions can almost always be cut with no loss of effect.

Yes, cut with no loss of effect.

Remember, every chapter, every page, every paragraph, every sentence, and every word needs to pull its weight. Repetitions like this don't hold up. No, they just don't.

Writing Tip #244: Stalling With "Started to"

I can just imagine it. The white page (or monitor) stares back at you. You type, "He started to . . . " and then you pause. What is your character going to do next? Your reader has no idea. Maybe you as the writer have no clue. The cursor blinks or your pen hangs poised until it comes to you.

When we write our early drafts, often there's a lot of fluff that allows the writing process to continue but that can be cleaned up at a later date. Here's the hint: remember to clean it up at a later date.

One example of a writer's brainstorming process that seems to linger far beyond when it should is the phrasing "started to" or "began to." He started to walk away. She started to laugh maniacally. The clouds started to turn gray. I say, why are you stalling? Let the man walk. Let the woman laugh. Let the clouds turn gray. There's no need for the extra words at the start of these sentences. They add no new information. They simply delay whatever is about to happen.

There are times when you need to note when something starts, but this isn't nearly as often as you might think. There's the expression "cut to the chase." Forget about the starting line unless it serves some greater purpose. Quit stalling, and let the action commence.

Writing Tip #245: Pronoun Clarity

If Eleanor Roosevelt and Wonder Woman walked into a bar (stay with me, folks), and she drank a beer in an iced-tea glass, do you know who "she" is? How's that for a grammatical riddle with some feminism on the side?

Besides the fact that I really wish I could join this duo and be the mysterious "she" in that sentence, the pronoun remains confusing. There are two women. Which one is the "she"?

I bring up this fabulously fictional scenario to illustrate a point. Be careful with your pronouns. Yes, we could discuss personal pronouns, demonstrative pronouns, relative, reflexive, indefinite, and even their antecedents, but I'm not going there.

He, him, she, her, it, you, they, them, who, whom, etc.—you know them; you love them; you use pronouns all the time. Just make sure you always use them with clarity. These little words can cause confusion far beyond any scenarios that begin with walking into a bar.

Oh, and speaking of that bar . . .

The answer to my riddle dives into some history. When Prohibition ended and Eleanor Roosevelt took on the task of reintroducing moderate alcohol consumption at the White House, she insisted on serving beer in iced-tea glasses; however, Roosevelt was also defined by her childhood as the daughter of an alcoholic and never touched it. Thus, the beer at the bar was clearly suggested by Roosevelt and drank by Wonder Woman.

And I still want to join them.

Cheers, everyone!

Writing Tip #246: "Fictional" Novels

Are you writing a fictional novel? Really? Is there a book inside of the book that you're writing? Confused? Yes, I think you might be.

This tip goes out to all of the fiction writers out there and really anyone who enjoys a good made-up story. Here it is, nice and simple:

Never describe a book as a "fictional novel."

Why? Because all novels are fiction. You're professionalism will go down a notch when you use this phrasing, and as a writer pushing ahead with your career, that's never something you want.

If you're talking about a "fictional novel," the literal translation is that you're talking about a book that was made up inside of a book. Think about it: a fictional character is a made up person in a story. A fictional book is the same thing. (See the Writing Tip #66: "Fictional" vs. "Fictitious" for further clarification.)

Gone Girl fans might remember the fictional novel "Amazing Amy." "The Heart is a Milkman" is a fictional novel inside of *Atlas Shrugged*. "The Mad Tryst" is a fictional novel inside of Edgar Allan Poe's "The Fall of the House of Usher." I'm sure J.K. Rowling probably had some good fictional novels in the Harry Potter series to complement the world of wizardry textbooks and "Beedle and the Bard" tales. Do I need to go on?

I know you want to sound savvy, but remember, especially if you're talking to book people—be they readers, editors, or literary agents—tell them all about your novel, not the imaginary one inside the one you're actually writing. It's not meta. It's just naïve.

Writing Tip #247: Misplaced Modifiers

Misplaced modifiers sound like items lost in the laundry. Somehow, you always lose a sock and a darn modifier ends up in the wrong location. No? Let's try this again.

Grammar terminology intimidates for some reason. Why, I'm not quite sure, but it may go back to strict English teachers in our formative years. Misplaced modifiers are actually quite simple to understand. A modifier is a word or phrase that modifies (or describes) something. A misplaced modifier is when that descriptor seems to be describing the wrong thing.

That sounds silly, right? Sure. But it happens all the time.

Glistening in the morning sun, the fisherman cast his line out to the water. (Did you catch the misplaced modifier? The "water" is "glistening in the morning sun," not the "fisherman.")

The hunter crouched in hiding waiting for a deer to come along with a bow and arrow. (Wait . . . who had the bow and arrow?)

Misplaced modifiers can be subtle, confusing, or funny, but be careful with your language. Of all the things we misplace, our ideas shouldn't be one of them.

Writing Tip #248: I Wonder About Punctuation?

Punctuation around the word "wonder" seems to commonly baffle writers. I wonder what the source of this is? (See what I did there? It's wrong. Did you notice?)

Reminder: just because something raises a question does not mean that it is a question. Think long and hard about that question mark.

Statements that begin with "I/she/he wonders . . . " are most commonly just that. Statements. There is no question about whether or not the subject wonders.

For example:

- I wonder why the sky is blue.
- She wonders whether the premise of *Mr. Popper's Penguins* is attainable with her refrigerator.
- He wonders if it would work with a pet seal if the fridge was big enough.

Do you see how all of these sentences bring up questions, but none of these sentences are questions themselves? Ergo, no question mark is needed. A plain old period is the perfect punctuation.

When someone wonders, let them ponder the mysteries of the universe, let them speculate and deliberate, but don't let the question return to your comprehension of proper punctuation.

Writing Tip #249: Starting Sentences with a Conjunction

Psst . . . I have a secret your old high school English teacher didn't want you to know. It's okay to begin with "And" or "But."

Admittedly, there's a good reason your English teachers didn't want you starting sentences with a conjunction. Developing strong writing skills is all about learning clarity and precision (see more on this Writing Tip #190), and academic writing especially requires a certain language formality—the same formality that requires the proper usage of who versus whom and semicolons (for more on these, see Writing Tips #206, #149, and #154). When students grow up and write professional correspondences, being in the habit of starting sentences in ways other than a conjunction will be a benefit to them.

But, of course, avoiding conjunctions at the start of sentences isn't a hard rule. If you're writing for a professional audience, an academic audience, or perhaps your grandmother, don't do it. However, in other cases, a well-placed conjunction at the start of a sentence can be an effective attention grabber.

And it's a bit more savvy than jazz hands or spirit fingers (oh, you know you get the *Bring It On* reference; don't deny it).

Starting sentences with a conjunction is an art of moderation. If you do it too often, your writing comes off as sloppy or unorganized. If you do it infrequently, though, that "and," "or," or "but" can pack a mean literary punch.

There are a lot of hard rules we were once taught that don't always apply. (For example, a well-placed sentence fragment is a personal favorite of mine. Really.) The difference is knowing the rules before you can break them. My argument is that, with self-control, you can absolutely use conjunctions at the start of a sentence.

Go for it, you grammar-rebel. And have fun.

Writing Tip #250: Balancing Dialogue, Action, and Description

Doctors argue that you should have a balanced diet, and I argue that you need to have balanced writing in your creative projects. The nutritionists say you need your proteins, your fruits, your veggies, and your grains. You cannot have a healthy body if you pick one food and focus on only that for a long duration of time. The same goes with balancing your story elements. You may have a weakness for delicious descriptions, but the body of your work will become weaker if that's all you put into it.

When you have a talent for something, it's fun to let it shine, but when you're a writer, you have to keep yourself in check. Some people are masters of dialogue. Others are poets when it comes to description.

Still others can keep readers holding their breath with the twists and turns of the action. However, not one of these people will find success if they don't work to balance all story elements within a project.

- If clever dialogue quips away but a reader has no sense of the characters, their physical relationship to each other, or their surroundings, it's like hearing words against the backdrop of a blank movie screen.
- No matter how elegantly crafted the description, if it goes on for too long without any action or dialogue to balance it out, it would become tiresome.
- Even amidst the most explosive action scenes, if you don't enable readers to become attached to your protagonist, the battle can fall flat.

Writing well takes time and practice. There's an art to weaving together description with characters and setting and plot, making sure your moments of introspection are brief but poignant and your tangents don't wander too far.

Any given scene needs to see many intermingled story elements like any given day needs to see many types of food. This is how book babies grow up to be big and strong. And don't you want your projects to be able to flex their powerful literary muscles?

CONCLUSION

In closing, word choice matters. How you build your sentence with punctuation is about more than just decorating with ink squiggle confetti. Knowing the subtleties can make you stand out. They can take you a step ahead.

Writing is a part of our everyday lives, whether we admit it or not. We write because we have a love affair with language or simply because our jobs mandate it. We write because words have made us giggle ever since reading Dr. Seuss as a young child or because even though we always hated English class, we need others to respond to us with sincerity and respect.

Maybe our mistakes are not laziness so much as ignorance. Grammar naiveté. The intricacies of the English language are not always taught, after all—though they can make our nerves feel taut. So let's take up our pens and keyboards and begin a written revolution, getting things right once and for all. All for words and words for all (or something like that). Huzzah!

Inspired? Awesome. If not, no worries. You don't have to love writing to take it seriously. You simply have to treat your words with as much esteem as you want others to treat you.

Happy writing, everybody!

DOCUMENTATION

"Altar." Merriam-Webster, accessed September 1, 2016. www.merriam-webster.com/dictionary/altar.

"Alter." Merriam-Webster, accessed September 1, 2016. www.merriam-webster.com/dictionary/alter.

"Aloud." Merriam-Webster, accessed December 10, 2014. www.merriam-webster.com/dictionary/aloud.

"Anytime." Merriam-Webster, accessed February 23, 2016. www.merriam-webster.com/dictionary/anytime.

Ammer, Christine. *The American Heritage Dictionary of Idioms*, 2nd ed. Boston: Houghton Mifflin Harcourt, 2013.

Barnhart, Robert K., ed. *The Barnhart Dictionary of Etymology: The Core Vocabulary of Standard English*. New York: H. W. Wilson Company, 1988.

Barratt, Leslie. "What Speakers Don't Notice: Language Changes Can Sneak In." *Virtuality and New Knowledge Structures*, Trans. *Internet-Zeitschrift für Kulturwissenschaften* 6 (2006).

Batt, Helene, and Kate Torgovnick May. "40 brilliant idioms that simply can't be translated literally." TED Blog, last modified January 20, 2015. http://blog.ted.com/40-idioms-that-cant -be-translated-literally/.

Beasley, Maurine Hoffman, Holly Cowan Shulman, and Henry
    R. Beasley. *The Eleanor Roosevelt Encyclopedia*. Westport, CT:
    Greenwood Publishing Group, 2001.

"The Birth of the Web." CERN, accessed October 17, 2016. https://
    home.cern/topics/birth-web.

"By and Large." Merriam-Webster, accessed October 1, 2016.
    www.merriam-webster.com/dictionary/by%20and%20large.

Carter, Ronald, Michael McCarthy, Geraldine Mark, and Anne
    O'Keeffe. *English Grammar Today: An A–Z of Spoken and Written
    Grammar*. Cambridge: Cambridge University Press, 2011.

Clark, Arthur Hamilton. *The Clipper Ship Era: An Epitome of Famous
    American and British Clipper Ships, Their Owners, Builders,
    Commanders, and Crews, 1843-1869*. New York: G.P. Putnam's
    Sons, 1912.

"Due Diligence." Merriam-Webster, accessed October 5, 2016.
    www.merriam-webster.com/dictionary/due%20diligence.

"Facts About Color Blindness." Department of Health and Human
    Services, The National Institutes of Health, accessed October 11,
    2016. https://nei.nih.gov/health/color_blindness/facts_about.

Frost, Robert. "Lodged." *West-Running Brook*. New York: Henry
    Holt, 1928.

Garner, Bryan A. *Garner's Modern American Usage: The Authority on
    Grammar, Usage, and Style*, 3rd ed. Oxford: Oxford University
    Press, 2009.

Grobel, Lawrence. *Conversations With Capote*. 1st ed. New York:
    Dutton, 1985.

Hacker, Diana. *A Writer's Reference*. 6th ed. Boston: Bedford/
    St. Martin's, 2007.

Houston, Keith. "The Ancient Roots of Punctuation." *The New Yorker*,
    last modified September 6, 2013. www.newyorker.com
    /books/page-turner/the-ancient-roots-of-punctuation.

Keats, John. "Isabella; or The Pot of Basil." *The Poetical Works of John
    Keats*. 2nd ed. Oxford: Oxford University Press, 1956.

Kirszner, Laurie G., and Stephen R. Mandell. *The Concise Wadsworth Handbook*. Boston: Thompson Wadsworth, 2005.

Martin, Emmie, Christina Sterbenz, and Melia Robinson. "The 17 strangest laws in America." *Business Insider*, last modified March 6, 2015. www.businessinsider.com/strangest-most-ridiculous -laws-in-america-2015-3.

"The meaning and origin of the expression: Spill the beans." *The Phrase Finder*, accessed August 2, 2016. www.phrases.org .uk/meanings/spill-the-beans.html.

Morford, Mark P.O., and Robert J. Lenardon. *Classical Mythology*. 6th ed. Boston: Addison-Wesley Educational Publishers Inc., 1999.

National Dictionary of the English Language: Based on the Principles Established by Noah Webster and Including a Practical Guide to Business English. New York: P.F. Collier & Son Corporation, 1940.

"Notorious." Merriam-Webster, accessed May 7, 2014. www.merriam-webster.com/dictionary/notorious.

O'Conner, Patricia T. *Woe Is I: A Grammarphobe's Guide to Better English in Plain English*. New York: G.P. Putnam's Sons, 1996.

"Out Loud." Merriam-Webster, accessed December 10, 2014. www.merriam-webster.com/dictionary/out%20loud.

Random House Webster's College Dictionary. New York: Random House, 1992.

Safire, William. *On Language*. New York: Times Books, 1980.

Safire, William. "On Language: Broaching the Telltale Brooch." *The New York Times Magazine*, 8 March 1998.

Safire, William. "On Language: Return of the Mondegreens." *The New York Times Magazine*, 23 January 1994.

"Usage Notes: Should you use 'dived' or 'dove'?" Merriam-Webster, accessed May 10, 2016. www.merriam-webster.com/words -at-play/dived-or-dove-which-is-correct.

"U.S. Navy Style Guide." America's Navy, accessed September 18, 2016. www.navy.mil/submit/view_styleguide.asp.

"What is the origin of the word 'OK'?" Oxford Dictionaries, accessed
    September 24, 2016. https://en.oxforddictionaries.com/explore
    /what-is-the-origin-of-the-word-ok.
"Word Fact: What's the Difference Between 'Discreet' and
    'Discrete'?" Merriam-Webster, last modified September 4, 2014.
    http://blog.dictionary.com/discreet-and-discrete/.
"Words at Play: Sneaked or Snuck: Which Is Correct?" Merriam-
    Webster, accessed September 29, 2016. www.merriam
    -webster.com/words-at-play/snuck-or-sneaked-which-is-correct.

INDEX